PEACE WITHOUT MONEY,
WAR WITHOUT AMERICANS

To my husband Aberu.

While everyone else was talking about the pivot to Asia, he pivoted to Europe and followed me from Taiwan to Brussels to marry me. Three years later, you still make it feel like we are newlyweds.

Peace Without Money,
War Without Americans

Can European Strategy Cope?

SVEN BISCOP
*Egmont – Royal Institute for International Relations, Belgium
and Ghent University, Belgium*

ASHGATE

Published by
Ashgate Publishing Limited
Wey Court East
Union Road
Farnham
Surrey, GU9 7PT
England

Ashgate Publishing Company
110 Cherry Street
Suite 3-1
Burlington, VT 05401-3818
USA

www.ashgate.com

British Library Cataloguing in Publication Data
A catalogue record for this book is available from the British Library.

The Library of Congress Catologing-in-Publication Data has been applied for

ISBN 9781472442888 (hbk)
ISBN 9781472442918 (pbk)
ISBN 9781472442895 (ebk – PDF)
ISBN 9781472442901 (ebk – ePUB)

Printed in the United Kingdom by Henry Ling Limited,
at the Dorset Press, Dorchester, DT1 1HD

Contents

About the Author

Prof. Dr. Sven Biscop is the director of the Europe in the World programme at the Egmont – Royal Institute for International Relations in Brussels, which he joined in 2002. Sven teaches at Ghent University and at the College of Europe in Bruges. As a member of the Executive Academic Board of the European Security and Defence College (ESDC), he regularly lectures in its courses, as well as in various European staff colleges, and at the People's University in Beijing, where he is a Senior Research Associate of the Centre for European Studies. Sven chairs the jury of the biennial European Defence Agency – Egmont PhD Prize in European Defence, Security & Strategy. In July 2015, Sven was made an Honorary Fellow of the ESDC, on the occasion of its tenth anniversary

List of Abbreviations

AGS	Alliance Ground Surveillance System
BG	Battlegroup
CDP	Capability Development Plan
CFI	Connected Forces Initiative
CFSP	Common Foreign and Security Policy
CSDP	Common Security and Defence Policy
DCFTA	Deep and Comprehensive Free Trade Agreement
DDR	Disarmament, Demobilization and Reintegration
DG	Directorate-General
EATC	European Air Transport Command
EDA	European Defence Agency
EEAS	European External Action Service
EEC	European Economic Community
EIB	European Investment Bank
EMP	Euro-Mediterranean Partnership
ENI	European Neighbourhood Instrument
ENP	European Neighbourhood Policy
ESDC	European Security and Defence College
ESDP	European Security and Defence Policy
ESS	European Security Strategy
EUMC	European Union Military Committee
EUMS	European Union Military Staff
FNC	Framework Nations Concept
GCC	Gulf Cooperation Council
HHG	Helsinki Headline Goal
HR	High Representative
IMF	International Monetary Fund
IS	Islamic State
ISTAR	intelligence, surveillance, target acquisition and reconnaissance
NDPP	NATO Defence Planning Process
NGOs	non-governmental organizations
NRF	NATO Response Force
OSCE	Organization for Security and Cooperation in Europe
PESCO	Permanent Structured Cooperation
R2P	Responsibility to Protect
SCO	Shanghai Cooperation Organization
SSR	Security Sector Reform

TEU   Treaty on European Union
TTIP   Transatlantic Trade and Investment Partnership
TPP   Trans-Pacific Partnership
VJTF   Very High Readiness Joint Task Force
WMD   weapons of mass destruction

Preface

Can Europe become an autonomous strategic actor only when the US orders it to? "Sir, yes Sir! Autonomy, Sir!". To this Belgian author it seems a frustrating contradiction in terms. But what may not work in theory does work in practice: autonomy really is the order of the day for Europe. Just when Europe's neighbourhood is in turmoil, on its eastern as well as on its southern borders, the focus of American strategy is shifting away from Europe, to China and Asia – the US "pivot". Autonomy is thus being forced upon the Europeans, who are slowly becoming aware that vital interests require resolute action in their broad neighbourhood – by themselves, for nobody will automatically do it for them.

Britain and France were surprised at having to convince the US of the need to intervene in Libya in 2011, when Gaddafi was poised to crush the last remaining stronghold of the opposition, the city of Benghazi. Usually it is the other way around: the US trying to persuade its European allies that military action must be undertaken. The crisis in Mali in early 2013, when French forces launched a quick reaction to prevent Jihadist militias from overrunning the country's capital, Bamako, confirmed the picture. Washington will support European action – if and when Europe acts. The US expects Europe to take the initiative, at least in its own periphery. That really is – at least regional – strategic autonomy. And Europe does exercise it. After Russia's annexation of the Crimea in 2014 and its successive incursion into eastern Ukraine, American deterrence, through the North Atlantic Treaty Organization (NATO), reassured European allies that their own territory was safe from a direct Russian threat. But it is Europe, under German leadership, that is trying to resolve the dispute with Russia, through diplomacy and sanctions.

Europe's newly acquired autonomy is constrained however by the aggravation of an old problem: lack of means. Under pressure of the financial crisis, defence budgets are (once more) being slashed across Europe, with just a very few exceptions, in spite of all the commitments that capitals have made to NATO, the European Union (EU), or both. Even in Britain and France, the continent's only real military powers in terms of strategic reflection and the will to deploy, defence budgets remain under pressure. And the military is but one instrument to be funded. Ideally Europe need not resort to the use of force at all, if the many other political and economic instruments that a truly comprehensive strategy for the broader neighbourhood requires are effective. Yet, to the south, the ramifications of the Arab Spring and still, the 2003 American invasion of Iraq and, to the east, the consolidation of democracy and good governance in Ukraine pose challenges of an enormous scale. In times of austerity budgets of that scale cannot be allocated. Nor can Europe ignore challenges in other parts of the world. As a global trade power, security in Asia is as vital to the European economy as the stability of Europe's periphery.

Peace Without Money, War Without Americans: this is the double challenge then that European strategy-makers are facing. And that is why, yes, I do think that another book on European strategy is needed, in spite of Hugh Trevor-Roper's (1947, p. 149) warning that "Those who habitually deal in rhetoric sometimes find more matter for it than the subject affords".

As austerity limits Europe's means, and the US pivot to Asia limits the extent to which it can count on American means, it becomes ever more important to ensure that what means remain to Europe are used in the most relevant and most effective way. It becomes essential, in other words, to prioritize – and that is exactly what strategy is all about. "Gentlemen, we have run out of money. It is time to start thinking", to quote Sir Winston Churchill (who can always be quoted on anything, but certainly on strategy).[1] Making the best use of European means also implies maximizing synergies and ending the dispersal of Europe's foreign and security policy efforts. No single European state can aspire to replace American power and single-handedly address the geopolitical turmoil in Europe's neighbourhood. Or does any capital really believe that it can defend its interests and deal with the Ukraine crisis, or the Syria/Iraq crisis, alone? In the face of the major strategic challenges facing them today, the national interest actually compels European states to act collectively.

The platform to do so exists: the EU controls substantial means of its own and (unlike NATO) has a comprehensive range of instruments covering all dimensions of foreign and security policy, from aid and trade to diplomacy and the military. The main argument of this book is that, therefore, the EU is best placed by far to devise the collective European foreign and security policy that our geopolitical environment imposes upon the European states, now more than ever. Through the EU, Europeans have already even attempted to forge a grand strategy integrating all these dimensions of external action: the 2003 European Security Strategy (ESS) (European Council, 2003). That has not produced a clear enough prioritization however. Consequently, EU foreign and security policy has not sufficiently proved its added value, and most capitals continue to think in terms of national instead of collective European policies. It is pressing to revisit the 2003 EU strategy and decide on which priorities collective action is required to complement the foreign policies of the European states.

This is precisely what the High Representative, Federica Mogherini, has embarked upon. Following her presentation of a report on Europe's strategic environment and on whether the EU has the instruments to cope (Mogherini 2015b), the European Council in June 2015 mandated her to "continue the process of strategic reflection with a view to preparing an EU global strategy on foreign and security policy in

---

1   Unfortunately he was probably addressing only gentlemen at the time. Though the quote is also attributed to New Zealand physicist Sir Ernest Rutherford, in this book on strategy I choose to believe Churchill is the source.

close cooperation with Member States, to be submitted to the European Council by June 2016" (European Council, 2015). To this process, this book aims to offer a humble contribution.

The first chapter will address what can actually be expected from strategy at the European level, and what cannot, before addressing the crucial question: can Europeans still do it? Or have they forgotten the art of making strategy? The chapter will also outline what I see as the four priority areas in which collective European strategy is the most urgent today. With two of these I will then deal in more detail, because, on the one hand, they definitely require action in the short term but also, on the other hand, because they are closest to my own area of expertise. Chapter 2 will look into the complex and interrelated crises that together constitute the overarching challenge to the stability of Europe's immediate neighbourhood, because if Europeans cannot make it there, they will not make it anywhere. Chapter 3 will assess whether European militaries specifically are up to the task, and how the need for autonomy can be squared with maintaining a strong alliance with the US. First however, a prologue will sketch the problem, for if decision-makers cannot be convinced that there is a problem, they will not arrive at a solution.

I would never have arrived at a book had it not been for the support of my employer, the Egmont – Royal Institute for International Relations in Brussels. Egmont is a true think tank, because it allows its researchers to search, in whichever direction they want. I am most grateful to the institute, which hired me as a fresh doctor in 2002, to its current director-general, Marc Otte, and indirectly also to the Belgian foreign ministry that funds the institute, for the freedom and the platform that Egmont continues to offer me. I am as grateful to Ashgate, and to Rob Sorsby in particular, for accepting to publish a slightly different type of book; the closest thing to an academic book that a think-tanker can come up with. There is only one species though, academics, some of whom dwell in universities and some in think tanks, and there are a few even, like myself, who try to move in both habitats. Ultimately both sub-species ought to aim to say something useful about the world, which in the case of a political scientist, means something about policy, those that make it, and those that vote about it. And they should try to do so in a readable way: "Life is short, and those who will not take the trouble to write clearly cannot properly expect to be read", said Trevor-Roper (2014, p. 139) with his usual wit.

I warmly thank my academic mentor, Professor Rik Coolsaet from Ghent University, for setting me an example of the role that an academic can play. I thank him even more for being such a good friend. Equal thanks are due to another close friend, now a senior associate fellow at Egmont: Brigadier-General (ret.) Jo Coelmont. His enthusiasm and creativity are unparalleled, and make possible the permanent process of thesis – anti-thesis – synthesis when the two of us think together about issues of strategy. I dare no longer say which ideas were initially his and which mine. Four other co-conspirators and friends stand out: Professor Alexander Mattelaer, Professor Luis Simón and Daniel Fiott at the Vrije Universiteit Brussel, and James Rogers at the Baltic Defence College. Constant interaction with this gang of four, usually over a good meal, has led to more than one great leap forward in my thinking. They deserve additional praise for pulling me into social media and the twenty-first century, against all the odds, by inviting me to join them as co-editor of the blog European Geostrategy. Particular thanks go to Professor Jolyon Howorth from Yale, the doyen of the field of European strategy and defence to whom we all defer, and to Professor Anand Menon from King's College London, a challenging yet most agreeable sparring partner on many occasions, who most kindly agreed to read through the whole manuscript and offered their advice and encouragement.

Sven Biscop
Brussels, 2015

Prologue
Snow White and the Seven Fallacies

EU strategy, European foreign policy: the words do not conjure up any grand images. In the absence, it seems, of any real ambition, there are neither triumphs to celebrate nor disasters to mourn. There is only gentle irrelevance to contemplate. Such is the image of Europe as an international player today in the minds of those who make and study foreign policy and strategy, in Europe's own as well as in foreign capitals. *Gentle* irrelevance, for Europe proclaims to wish the world well and it is generous enough with its money to prove it. Not throwing military power around it presents no cause for fear, only for irritation, in some corners, with its inconvenient insistence on universal values. But *irrelevance* nonetheless, for Europe lacks the unity and sense of purpose for resolute and sustained action to uphold these values, and continues to liberally spend its money quite regardless of values or effect. Increasingly irrelevant even, for in the wake of the financial crisis Europe struggles to maintain its own model of society, which undermines the legitimacy of its value-based narrative and erodes the will as well as the means for external action.

Even if the image was false (and alas it is not, at least not entirely), because of it Europe is treated with benign neglect, by those that take its money, by its supposed "strategic partners" among the emerging powers, and even by its allies, the US above all. All of them go through the motions of meetings and summits without really considering Europe a force to be taken into account. Many have been quick to exploit the absence of purposive action on the part of Europe to occupy the ground (the seas, the resources, the hearts and minds…) that Europe has abandoned or not cared to occupy. Europe, in sum, is not perceived and therefore not treated as a strategic actor, as a pole of the multipolar world, as one of the great powers.

And yet there is ground for optimism, because this unsettling story is mostly of Europe's own making. The emerging powers are emerging and the world has become multipolar, so Europe's relative weight has declined. But its absolute weight in world politics could be much greater. The story could still have a happy end, if only the governments of Europe would see through the following seven fallacies that stop them from being the player that *collectively* they could be.

The Dwarfs

There are only two kinds of countries in Europe, Belgian statesman Paul-Henri Spaak is reputed to have said: small countries and those that have yet to realize that they are but that – small countries. Alas, the latter far outnumber the former. To believe that on the world stage any European state is more than a dwarf is the single most damning fallacy for Europe's global role, for it creates the illusion in many capitals that they do not need the other Europeans.

It particularly stimulates bilateral wheeling and dealing with the great powers (the US, Russia and China especially) to the detriment of collective European engagement, which is seen as no more than a secondary supplement to national foreign policy. It creates a competition between Europeans to appear the most attractive to investment by and trade with the great powers; in practice that often translates as being the most compliant. *Divide et impera*: Europeans divide themselves and the great powers rule. For the great powers would not long remain great powers without a certain degree of cunning: of course they play off one European state against the other, since they offer them the opportunity on a silver platter. Europeans even go to the extent of acting collectively to undermine their own collective institutions: since 2012 for example Europe has allowed the emergence of a separate diplomatic track between China and Central and Eastern Europe, alongside the formal EU–China strategic partnership. What the 16 European states involved stand to gain, apart from the fleeting illusion of importance, is not quite clear – that China stands to gain from this arrangement need not be doubted for a moment.

This fallacy is understandable, for some dwarfs do carry a big sword and others do possess a big purse. But dwarfs being dwarfs, it is either/or: no single European state today can claim global reach in all dimensions of power, military, economic, and political. Therefore some states can defend their interests alone some of the time, but no single European state can defend all of its interests on its own all of the time. Surely no European country assumes it can deal alone with all the ramifications of the Arab Spring, to name just the obvious example. None has the military clout: Britain and France could initiate the interventions in Libya and Mali in 2011 and 2013 (and deserve our appreciation for it) but could not see them through without assistance from the US and from other Europeans. Nor does any European government have the financial means.

The conclusion is obvious: because some threats and challenges are just too big to face alone, in many instances defending the national interest demands collective action. Then why do they not do it?

Snow White

To convince the Member States of the need for collective action through the EU, the Union must prove it can more effectively defend those interests which its Member States individually can no longer safeguard. Unfortunately, for a long time many officials and observers regarded interests as a notion that does not or should not apply to the EU. The pursuit of interests runs contrary to their idealized view of an altruistic EU foreign policy. This is the attitude that leads some to condemn the interventions in Libya and Mali for the mere fact that they served our interests. One wonders whether these critics think any government would put its soldiers at risk when they have no interest at all in the matter, and whether they do not think that the people of Libya and Mali feel that the interventions at the same time were very much in their interest too. They accept that states have national interests, of course, and that the Commission's DG Trade defends interests is somehow acceptable too. But the EU's Common Foreign and Security Policy (CFSP) in this view exists solely to do good in the world: the EU as Snow White, pure, innocent – and helpless.

That is another fallacy, for union should create strength, not weakness. *L'union fait la force*: not all Belgians may feel that their Kingdom's motto does or should apply to their country, but it certainly applies to Europe.

Fortunately, attitudes are evolving. For example the EU's anti-piracy operation in the Gulf of Aden, Atalanta, was always publicly motivated by a desire to protect UN food shipments and to assist the people of Somalia – a laudable purpose of course – while referring to the protection of European trade initially was "not done", as if the one excludes the other. This is the atmosphere in which in 2010 German president Horst Köhler resigned after facing a barrage of criticism over his remarks (speaking about Afghanistan) that German military deployments serve German economic interests. Well of course! The real reason why Operation Atalanta continues to this day is of course that Europe's commercial shipping passes by there – but that does not mean that it does not serve the interests of Somalia at the same time. Today however, EU officials proudly refer to Atalanta as the first military operation under the EU's Common Security and Defence Policy (CSDP) that was specifically designed to protect European interests. The European External Action Service (EEAS), the EU's diplomatic service, even organizes official seminars in Washington, Beijing and Ottawa to pass on the message that "we can do it too", that the EU can be a strategic actor if it wants to.

The need to focus EU foreign policy on interests is now acknowledged at the highest political level. At the December 2012 meeting of the European Council, i.e. the Heads of State and Government of the 28 EU Member States, they noted that "in today's changing world the European Union is called upon to assume increased responsibilities in the maintenance of international peace and security in order to guarantee the security of its citizens and *the promotion of its interests* [emphasis added]". In a report to the European Council in late 2013, the then High Representative, Catherine Ashton, called for a Union able "to act decisively as a security provider" and "to protect its interests" (Ashton, 2013). Her successor, the current High Representative Federica Mogherini, put it even more clearly:

> I believe any narrative of a clash among national interests and European interests is flawed. We hold a "joint place in the world", and it very much depends on the unity and the effectiveness of the European Union's international projection. It should be clear to everyone that we, the Europeans, are much better when we are together. It is a matter not of European interest but of national interest, for all. (Mogherini, 2015a)

Foreign policy is about interests. The recognition at the EU level that that simple fact is neither good nor bad is the first step towards a Union of strength. It is the way in which these interests are then pursued that can be "good" or "bad"; that indeed requires close scrutiny. Sometimes even the "good" way will require the use of force, though. Let us not forget that Europe's vital interests include upholding the core of international law, notably the illegality of war and the "Responsibility to Protect" people from genocide, ethnic cleansing, war crimes and crimes against humanity (a principle voted by the United Nations General Assembly in 2005). In such situations, civilian power alone quickly leaves one powerless, for power is the result of a multiplication of factors: if one factor (military, economic or political/civilian) equals zero, the end result equals zero too (Coelmont, 2009, p. 23).

Of course force should remain the last resort. But a Union that is *never* willing to apply force under its own flag will never be a credible platform for collective action to those of its members that have a strong strategic culture that includes the active use of the military instrument.

The Apple

If European foreign policy is about interests, more is called for than going around the world handing out free apples in return for a token commitment to human rights and democracy. It is another fallacy to equate foreign policy with taking part in programmes and projects. Programmes are continued because they existed last year, the budget was spent, and has been allocated again. Too many EU "policy" decisions amount to extending or adding to existing budget lines, without setting clear objectives or even assessing the effectiveness of past programmes. European foreign policy often is not political enough.

Europe's reaction to the turmoil in its southern neighbourhood that followed the Arab Spring is a prime example. The initial formal policy response in 2012, which the EU called "More for More", in reality amounted to more of the same: extra money was allocated to the existing European Neighbourhood Policy (ENP), the framework in which since 2004 the EU organizes relations with its immediate neighbours to the south as well as the east, but without reassessing its objectives and instruments. Why would a policy that did not yield results in the seven years before the Arab Spring, all of a sudden work now? The additional money definitely was in any case not enough to make a difference. Under the ENP the EU has substantial means to spend: €100 or €200 million per country per year. But one cannot go to Cairo with a few €100 million and announce that one will take the country in hand. For one, Saudi Arabia would step in and just add another zero to that amount. More importantly, the economic challenge in a country like Egypt is obvious, but it is so huge that it is beyond Europe's means to address it in one fell swoop. As an American commentator phrased it: "A Marshall Plan here and a Marshall Plan there and soon you're talking about real money" (Coll, 2013).

In any case, more money will not generate more effect if the way it is used remains unaltered. Conditionality – handing out apples to the good pupils – is less and less effective. Other actors, like China, have a huge apple basket too, so Europe's relative leverage declines, especially because Beijing imposes far less stringent conditions (at least when it comes to human rights and democracy). More importantly, this basically paternalistic approach is no longer in touch with the times. Particularly in countries where people have just taken their fate into their own hands, or have tried to, like in Tunisia, Egypt and Libya, they now want to craft their own model, rather than passively adopting a model from the outside, be it from Europe or elsewhere.

In its desire to be liked by everybody, like Snow White, Europe has declared partnership with just about everybody, with the emerging powers, with all of its neighbours, and many more, promising them apples if they would only become like Europe itself: democratic social market economies that guarantee the security, prosperity, freedom and equality of their citizens. In practice, by formally accepting regimes as partners even before they changed, the EU has taken away much of the incentive for change and has reduced its own freedom of action. For once partnership has been announced, it is difficult for Europe to keep its distance and remain critical – Snow White is not the one to be strict and cut off the apple supply when necessary. As a result, rather than changing Europe's partners, the whole notion of partnership has been tainted by the inclusion of unsavoury regimes which in the public eye became Europe's friends. The apple has proved to be poisonous: neither the one that gave it nor the one that accepted it is much the better for it.

Time to abandon programmes and partnerships and return to diplomacy. Partnership is for those with whom Europe does share respect for the same universal values on which its own model of society is based and with whom therefore it can systematically engage in joint *action*. With others, Europe can have diplomatic relations that allow for a *dialogue* and, if that is successful, occasional cooperation on specific issues. The EU is good at diplomacy, actually. It was the EU that kept the negotiations with Iran about the nuclear file going, for many years, until finally the US came to the table. It was the EU, likewise, that brokered the Minsk II agreement to try and end the war in Ukraine, disregarding more belligerent voices impatiently calling for more arms deliveries to Kiev. In neither case has a final settlement been achieved at the time of writing, but it is clear that without the EU there would not even be a chance of a diplomatic solution.

The Witch

Once again the question can be asked: why then does the Union not live up to its potential? If misfortune befalls Snow White, we blame the witch. But this is another fallacy: it is all too easy to blame someone else for the ineffectiveness of EU foreign policy, but in the end most of the blame lies with the Member States themselves, who are not willing to let the EU play the role that it could play.

The programmatic approach to foreign policy is often decried as the result of the dominance of the ways of the Commission within the EEAS (the officials of which come from the Commission, from the Council as well as from national foreign ministries). But if that is to some extent true, it only holds sway because too many Member States are too exclusively focussed on their national foreign policies and do not sufficiently use the collective EU instruments and institutions (that they have themselves created). "More for More", to stay with the same example, is too programmatic by far, but it was also quite surprising that no Member State seemed to push for a really new policy towards the southern neighbours, or even just for a real reassessment of the ENP (until the EU finally launched a review process in March 2015).

Blaming the previous High Representative, Ashton, for the lack of success of EU external action was a favourite Brussels pastime. This author must admit to having joined the chorus of criticism on more than one occasion, notably because of the absence of strategic debate and lack of prioritization and initiative. But Kissinger himself, for all his criticism of Europe ("What is Europe's phone number?"), would not be able to take any grand initiative if confronted with a *fronde* of unable and unwilling presidents and ministers, who are concerned more with the prestige that national policies can bring than with the ineffectiveness resulting from a lack of European policies. He had to deal with only one Nixon, after all. No High Representative can make policy against the Member States – they have to work with the capitals, and the capitals have to be willing to work with them. When Mogherini took up her position in late 2014, people were so fed up with the air of negativity that in the end hung about her predecessor that everyone was longing for a constructive atmosphere – hopefully that constructive spirit can be maintained.

Finally, if all else fails, one can always blame the Chinese or, depending on the dossier, the Russians, for the absence of success. But while they do often undermine EU policy, capitals forget that they make it all too easy for them to do so if they are too divided to devise an unambiguous policy themselves. In the field, resolute *strategy* usually wins out over mere wishy-washy *presence*.

The Prince

More important than shouldering (much of) the blame, is assuming responsibility. Member States will have to assume a lot more responsibility, for what was the bedrock of European strategic thinking has now also become a fallacy: Europe can no longer count on its prince from America to come and save it from each and every danger. Not that the prince does not care for Europe anymore: if once again the territory of Europe itself were directly threatened, he would charge to the rescue, because that directly concerns American vital interests. But in the absence of such a threat, the real focus of US strategy is now on Asia and the Pacific. Princes have a thing with dragons after all – fair maidens like Snow White tend to get boring if a maiden they intend to stay. Consequently, in case of crises in Europe's broad neighbourhood

Washington expects Europe to take the initiative and respond with its own means, at an early stage, with US support in specific areas (notably intelligence), in order to prevent escalation and the drawing in of more substantial US assets.

US action in recent crises in Europe's southern periphery bears out the reality of this "pivot", not so much of American military assets (most US combat troops had already been redeployed) but of the focus of American strategy. The intervention in Libya in 2011 was still more of an American operation in a European guise. Europeans for the greater part had to rely on American strategic enablers (precision guided munitions, air-to-air refuelling, intelligence) without which they would have faced great difficulties to run such an air campaign, but Europeans initiated and had to convince the US of the need of the intervention rather than the other way around. And the American message afterwards was clear: Europeans ought to be able to wage such a campaign, of after all limited size, and on their doorstep, alone. One can hardly disagree. The 2013 intervention in Mali conformed much more with American expectations: Europeans initiated an intervention and saw it through with US involvement largely limited to intelligence. Even the major US role in addressing the civil war in Syria (and afterwards Iraq, again) testifies to the reality of the "pivot", because it is a role which it did not seek. When President Barack Obama publicly declared the use of chemical weapons to be a red line beyond which the US could not remain inactive, this was a polite way of saying that the US was *not* going to get involved in the conflict, since the calculation in Washington clearly was that nobody would be foolish enough to cross this line. Alas, once a red line is drawn, one can always count on someone to step over it; hence the US was drawn in against its intention. The crisis on Europe's eastern borders is even more indicative of the new American mind-set: Washington has to address it, but sees it more as an unfortunate distraction than as a priority in its own right.

The implication is clear: those European governments that are still denying the reality of the shift in American strategy, intimating that we have seen and heard it all before, are engaging in a dangerous exercise of wishful thinking. "Before" was during the Cold War, when the European front in any case was central to US strategy; today the US sees China as its most important strategic competitor. Europeans may be justified in preferring not to think in such terms about China, for designating enemies can easily become a self-fulfilling prophecy. But they cannot escape the consequences of the fact that the Americans do: Europe *will* sometimes be on its own. Denial of this unpleasant (but entirely logical) fact of life is not going to help Europe prepare for it.

Unfortunately, few of the recent crises have really been addressed by Europe collectively. In Libya and Mali, intervention was initiated and implemented by ad hoc coalitions; the EU came in only afterwards. In Libya it came in far too late; as a result, the effect created by the military intervention was negated and the country sank back into civil war. In Mali the EU did arrive sooner, with a fully-fledged comprehensive strategy, and results have proved to be much more lasting. On Syria, EU sanctions had been imposed early on, but at heart Member States differed decisively about the way to deal with the war: arming or at least otherwise supporting the forces of the opposition, in order to safeguard influence after the hoped for fall of the Assad regime, or continuing to sit on the fence, for fear of handing power to jihadist elements now dominant in the very much divided rebel camp. The picture changed entirely when the self-proclaimed Islamic State (IS) conquered large swaths of territory in Syria and Iraq, thus making them into one theatre. But even then only some Europeans deployed their air forces and/or trainers to Iraq.

In all these cases, Britain and/or France were at the core of (attempts to create) ad hoc coalitions that undertook a "European" action, which after the facts inevitably drew in the EU, which alone has the political and economic instruments and means for post-intervention stabilization. This is not a viable model for the long term. On the one hand, neither Britain nor France can seriously hope to supplant US power and always bear the greatest share of the burden of European military action – they simply no longer have the means. On the other hand, a Union in which Paris and London perennially decide when and where to intervene, while the other Member States can decide to join or to abstain but do not have real influence on French and British decision-making (just like Europe as a whole has little impact on American decisions of war and peace) is not tenable.

Furthermore, when dealing with the Ukraine crisis, Germany rather than Britain or France turned out to be the leading European actor. When Germany, which has the most important economic relationship with Russia of all EU Member States, took a hard stance on sanctions, the others had to follow. Chancellor Angela Merkel showed considerable skill and leadership in trying to forge a diplomatic solution, mediating (together with French President François Hollande) the Minsk II agreement with Russian President Vladimir Putin in February 2015. The UK was notably absent from the high table. Berlin is of course understood to be acting on behalf of the 28, whose consent is vital to maintain sanctions.

The same conclusion is evident once again: collective action under the political aegis of the EU, guided by a focus on interests, is the only viable option. Soon enough, the choice will no longer be between national or collective action, but between collective action or no action at all.

The Castle

The prince's pivot exposes yet another fallacy: the CSDP and NATO are not competing castles in the same shire that should therefore be jockeying for influence – they are but wings of one and the same castle that defends the shire as a whole. Unfortunately, a fallacious focus on institutions has generated a reductionism that is detrimental to the quality of the European strategic debate. Nearly every issue is automatically reduced to the question of the desired competences and prestige of the preferred organization: the EU or NATO. Falsely perceived as a zero-sum game, it has led to a ridiculous beauty contest between NATO and the CSDP. Fighting Somali pirates? Europeans deploy on two separate operations, the EU's Atalanta and NATO's Ocean Shield. Joining multinational capability development efforts? Europeans engage in two separate schemes, the EU's Pooling & Sharing and NATO's Smart Defence. European governments are perfectly capable, furthermore, of defending contradictory positions on one and the same issue depending on whether they sit in a NATO or an EU meeting. Mirror, mirror on the wall, which is the mightiest security organization of them all?[1]

At a stroke, the US pivot has rendered this debate entirely obsolete. It is often presented as if the EU is divided but fortunately NATO at least always has a clear strategy and the will to act. In fact, *the US* usually has a strategy which it then, because the Europeans are indeed divided, imposes on NATO. But the US will not take the lead anymore in responding to crises in the European periphery; they expect Europe to take the lead and initiate a response. Without the preponderant US lead, NATO is nothing more, politically speaking, than that same quarrelling bunch of Europeans that also makes up the EU. The question is not therefore whether in a given crisis it is up to NATO or the CSDP to act, but whether *Europeans* will act. If they do, they will make use of NATO, or the CSDP, or other EU instruments, or, most likely, a combination thereof – the specific circumstances of each contingency will determine which instruments are apt and available to be put to use. If they do not, then nobody will make use of any of these, including NATO, whose great asset, its command and control structure, will just be sitting idle.

Whether Europeans act through NATO or the CSDP, in an increasing number of cases it will indeed be Europeans, alone, that will have to bear the brunt of the action. Trying to design a strict division of labour between NATO and the CSDP is a futile exercise therefore, because they are but instruments. One does not lay down in elaborate detail which competences one accords to the different tools in a toolbox – rather one tries to have as comprehensive a toolbox as possible and select the right combination of tools from it to address the problem that needs solving.

There are many instruments available in NATO, the CSDP, as well as in other parts of the EU, in the UN and at the national level, but there is only one Europe to serve. Logically, Europe ought to have one view on which instruments it needs and what it expects them to be able to do. Specifically, Europeans cannot have one view on intervention and the use of force when they meet in the EU and another when they meet in NATO. The then President of the European Council, Herman Van Rompuy, tried to steer Europe in the right direction when in 2012 he called for a debate among the Heads of State and Government (to be held in December 2013), not about the CSDP, but about "the state of defence in Europe". The crucial question to be answered, which has become rather urgent because of the US pivot, is: which responsibilities is *Europe* willing to assume as a security provider, regardless of whether in a specific case it will act through the CSDP or NATO or both. The

---

1   Credit for this image must go to Alexander Mattelaer, who clearly caught the author's vibe.

problem is that there is today no recognized forum where Europeans can meet and take decisions about their role in security and defence in both NATO and the EU – it is always either/or. The preparation of the December 2013 European Council proves how difficult it is to overcome the reductionist fallacy: even though Van Rompuy wanted it to be about "the state of defence in Europe", it was then prepared via the usual channels, i.e. EU channels, and thus ended up to be just about the CSDP after all. Fortunately, as we will see in later chapters, it did adopt some important decisions anyway.

The European Council is an EU body, of course, but they are the Heads of State and Government of the 28 Member States, meeting in an intergovernmental context, deciding by consensus, adopting not binding law but political declarations. Surely they could agree to state explicitly that they will regard their conclusions as political guidance for their governments' positions in both the EU and NATO. But before they can agree on anything, they need to have a thorough substantial debate. Dare one say: a strategic debate?

The Fairy Tale

This brings us neatly to the last fallacy: European governments will not be able to overcome any of the other fallacies if they continue to refuse to engage in the strategic debate. Precisely because they are so divided today, they need a fairy tale, a story-line, a narrative, to tie it all together and stipulate what it is that they want to do together: a strategy.

Europeans do not have to do everything together. The aim is not to upload everything to the collective European agenda. The point of strategy is precisely the opposite: it is to make choices, to set priorities. What Europe does not need is a compilation of all the priorities of all of the 28 national foreign policies; that would yield a Christmas tree but not a strategy that can be acted upon. Nor is there a need to say a little something about every imaginable subject of EU external action; we have www.europa.eu for that. An EU strategy for foreign policy or external action is to focus on a short list of key priorities, which all 28 Member States see as priorities, and on which collective action brings the greatest added value because none of the 28 can see them through on its own. Guiding all of Europe's collective external action for every five-year legislature (and term of office of the High Representative), this would be grand strategy – grand enough to also guide European positions in and on NATO when they use that instrument.

Europe may not be widely seen as a strategic actor, but most people in the world do agree that Europe is a good place to live. That points us to what Europe has achieved: through a unique combination of democracy, capitalism and "big government", it has created a much more equal society than can be found in most other places around the world, which provides the greatest security, prosperity and freedom to the greatest number of its citizens. But not yet to all of its citizens, so although this aspiration to equality is anchored in the Treaty on European Union, an aspiration it remains. Europe must take great care that in its eagerness to save the Euro, it does not destroy the social model which the Euro was meant to serve – not to threaten. It is the social model that binds citizens to the European *idea*, not the Euro: the intuition that even though one does not quite understand how it works, the EU is good for one's wellbeing. Europe is in great danger of arriving at the opposite: that people still do not understand how the EU works but feel that it threatens their wellbeing; in some Member States this undoubtedly already is the case, as the results of austerity policies having been pushed way too far.

The fairy tale does not start in a faraway land therefore, but has to start at home: Europe has a great deal of work ahead to consolidate and then to deepen its social model. At the same time, this internal strategic challenge is at the heart of Europe's external strategy. On the one hand, the conditions that have to be fulfilled for Europe to achieve this, its fundamental purpose, constitute its vital interests. The way to generate the priorities of a European grand strategy for foreign policy is to assess the global environment and identify the most important threats and challenges to these shared vital interests. Foreign policy is about interests, as stated above, but on the other hand, the European idea continues to shape the *way* Europeans pursue them: not as a zero-sum game, but in such a way that they try not to harm the legitimate interests of others. The best way of achieving international peace and security is to convince other governments to provide for the security, prosperity and freedom of their citizens just as European governments and the EU provide for theirs. Europe must be willing to use coercion and the use of force, or the credible threat of it, but only as a last resort.

The debate between capitals about the need to write a common fairy tale risked becoming a never-ending story, but fortunately a decision-point is in sight. When Federica Mogherini took up office as the new High Representative after the May 2014 European elections, she quickly established the priority of a strategic review. A new strategy is set to be adopted by June 2016. Is it not logical that every High Representative would start every five-year term with a clear set of priorities, in whichever form they are written down, or maybe just in a speech?

The Way out of the Forest

The EU has created first a Common Foreign and Security Policy and then a Common Security and Defence Policy. This is very much like states that call themselves Democratic Republics: the more the need is felt to explicitly stress how democratic or common something is, the more autocratic and divided it usually is in reality. There is no magic wand that will allow us to conjure up a European strategic consensus out of nowhere. But there is no reason for pessimism either. European governments cling to their prerogatives, but they are also pragmatic. We have seen in the wake of the Eurozone crisis that in spite of the initial national reflex of many capitals, and reluctant though they still may be, the agreed way out of the crisis is another step to European integration – a very big step even. The long-term trend towards ever closer Union thus continues. Slowly, because most Member States will not think of Europeanizing an issue area until the moment when they have no other options left – but then they will, including in foreign, security and defence policy. Perhaps quicker than we might expect, given the enormous pressure on defence budgets today.

So, will Europeans live happily ever after? The key is that in every fairy tale they live happily ever after *together*. How that can be achieved is the topic of the next chapters.

Chapter 1
Strategy-Making in Europe:
Raiders of the Lost Art

Nobody could predict the Arab Spring anyway, or the crisis in Ukraine, or the civil war in Syria, so why should one need strategy? One has no choice but to make it all up as one goes along, reacting to unpredictable events. Let us not waste time therefore on drafting strategic documents, which with 28 Member States around the table will be extremely difficult. This is still the view taken by many practitioners of foreign and security policy, both in the capitals and in Brussels. While it indicates an understandable frustration with often cumbersome and tedious negotiations, this position also betrays a fundamental misunderstanding about the function of strategy.

It is true that practitioners as well as academics rarely predict anything with any degree of success or precision. If one keeps predicting the same thing over and over again it may eventually come true, but that does not really count (and, in any case, people usually tire so quickly of Cassandras that even when they turn out to be right they are still ignored). In reality, the revolutions that are predictable are those that do not happen, for if I can foresee them watching from afar from my comfortable seat in a think tank or a university, then so can those who they seek to dethrone. But strategy does not aim to predict anything in the first place. The point of strategy, rather, is to help the decision-maker define a course of action when per definition unpredictable events occur. How important is this *for me*? That is the question that strategy will help answer, and that answer will determine whether and what action has to be undertaken and which means have to be allocated to it.

The first rule of strategy-making therefore could be stated quite simply as: know thyself. Know your interests, and know your values. Values and interests are not in contradiction: your values will determine which kind of society you want to build and preserve, and that will in turn determine which conditions need to be fulfilled for that to be possible: your vital interests. Your values will further determine which types of instruments are deemed morally acceptable to put to use to that end. Strategy-making then starts with an analysis of the world, in order to identify the most important threats and challenges to one's values and interests, so as to define ends, ways and means: setting priority objectives, choosing the instruments to achieve them, and allocating the necessary means.

Of course, when a crisis occurs and unpredictable events do turn out to be important because vital interests are directly at stake, urgency in combination with uncertainty and a lack of information will create friction. The fog of diplomacy or, in a worst case scenario, of war, is unavoidable. Yet that is still something different than mere improvisation, which is what decision-making without any prior strategy would amount to. To use a current example: Russian aggression against Ukraine would be seen in an entirely different light, and the response of the EU and NATO would be very different, had Europe not had the regional strategy that it has, the Neighbourhood Policy and the Eastern Partnership, and the strategic partnership with Russia. Similarly, the way Europeans understand and respond to the crises in their southern periphery are framed by the pre-existing southern Neighbourhood Policy and the Union for the Mediterranean with the southern littoral states. Best therefore to think about values and interest beforehand.

A fully-fledged strategic actor will not limit himself to reacting to events. He will also try and proactively shape events and developments. The other function of strategy therefore is to set out a limited number of overall objectives, in order to guide day-to-day decision-making and the allocation of the budget and other means. Finally, though some elements of strategy may remain secret, strategy also serves accountability and public diplomacy. It is a way of communicating how one sees one's role in the world, in order to legitimize one's actions *vis-à-vis* parliaments and citizens, and to create clarity *vis-à-vis* allies, partners and competitors alike. "Grand strategies are good for democracy" (Posen, 2014, p. 5).

Does one need to put all of that in writing? The more straightforward the decision-making system, the less necessary it is to codify strategy. A state where in the end the strategy is what the president (or the politburo) says that it is, can operate on the basis of an implicit strategy. Vice versa, a complex multi-layered foreign policy actor such as the EU has much more need of an explicit strategy, such as its 2003 European Security Strategy (ESS). The chance that the High Representative and 28 foreign ministers, not to mention the President of the European Council and 28 heads of state and government, all have the same implicit understanding of EU strategy is rather small. Freedman (2013, p. 614) is clear: "Not only does strategy need to be put into words so that others can follow, but it works through affecting the behaviour of others. Thus it is always about persuasion, whether convincing others to work with you or explaining to adversaries the consequences if they do not".

Documents like the ESS operate at the level of grand strategy (framing all dimensions of foreign policy or external action), and put forward broad long-term goals, which have to be translated into more specific functional and regional strategies. But such strategies do not remain valid for ever. Many of the policies that operate under the aegis of the ESS, and the Neighbourhood Policy is just one of them, have been overtaken by events. One cannot carry on as if there has been no Arab Spring, no Ukraine crisis, no US pivot, and no rise of China. A review of the overarching grand strategy, the ESS, is long overdue therefore. The new High Representative, Federica Mogherini, is to be commended for helping to break the deadlock in the official European strategic debate, which for years had been limited to the rather unproductive question: shall we or shall we not revisit the ESS? Finally, in June 2015 Mogherini was mandated to complete a new strategy by June 2016. Few Member States showed great enthusiasm even then, however. With a few exceptions, most capitals in the course of 2015 just rather grudgingly came to accept that a strategic review can no longer be postponed. One of the underlying reasons is that many European states are simply not used to making strategy anymore.

European Strategy: Implicit, Impeded, and Inevitable

Most if not all European states do have a certain concept of strategy. Even my own country, Belgium, counter-intuitive though it may be, has a grand strategy. Belgium may not use the term "grand strategy" or even just "strategy" in official parlance, but implicitly, subconsciously even, it does have one. History has taught that the powers of Europe either talk each other to death in Brussels meeting rooms or fight each other to death on Belgian battlefields. From a Belgian point of view, the choice is quickly made, hence its drive to promote European integration, especially among its immediate neighbours, France and Germany. That is now so engrained that it is rarely explicitly discussed; it has become part of Belgian strategic culture. But it is a grand strategy, for it concerns the very survival of the country. Seventy years after the end of World War Two the prospect of war among Belgium's neighbours seems remote, unimaginable even, but from the perspective of world history, it is but a short period. Just 14 years shorter, in fact, than the period that elapsed between the independence of Belgium in 1830 and its invasion in 1914. Deepening European integration remains a relevant grand strategy for Belgium's national security therefore. But it is hardly relevant to the crises around Europe, in its eastern and southern neighbourhoods, to give just one example. Belgian grand strategy is still linked to the national territory. But Belgium is now part of a single European market and of a currency union, hence it should worry about threats to the Union as a whole, which are acute, and not just about direct threats to its own territory, which are very unlikely.

Many EU Member States are in the same position as Belgium. Their historical experience has generated a deeply engrained strategic orientation: invasion and occupation for Belgium, the Winter War for Finland, partition and abandonment for Poland, defeat for Germany, etc. But they have not adapted their strategic thinking to the fact that as EU Member States what are indirect threats to their own territory are in fact direct threats against the Union – and therefore against themselves. For most of the Cold War, European capitals were actively incentivized not to think strategically: Washington or Moscow, depending on which side of the Iron Curtain they were on, did the strategizing for them and rather preferred not to have independent-minded allies. Few Member States have emancipated themselves from that mind-set of subservience, however, even though the Cold War is now more than a quarter century behind us.

The problem goes even deeper than that. Because European integration has been so successful that war between EU Member States has pretty much become a practical impossibility, within the Union geopolitics and defence do not really matter any longer. As a result, many capitals have forgotten how to think in geopolitical terms altogether. Unfortunately, this impairs their analysis of the world around the EU, even if they were to attempt to address it strategically, where most actors do still think in exactly such terms. For most capitals outside Europe, Stalin's question – "How many divisions has the pope?" – remains very acute. If Europeans do not realize that, they will never be able to correctly analyse their own strategic situation.

The exceptions are of course Britain and France. As nuclear powers and permanent members of the UN Security Council they have maintained a global outlook and an expeditionary posture in their armed forces as well as military bases across the globe. Both countries have a strategic culture in which the use of force is an acceptable instrument of statecraft, and both have an intricate national strategic process, producing regular defence reviews and white books to give direction to their military instrument. But while British and French thinking does not suffer from the same self-imposed limitations as that of most other Europeans, their means to implement whichever strategy they elaborate have become very limited indeed. Possessing a nuclear deterrent, Paris and London are confident that they can defend the national territory. But neither France nor the UK alone can have any significant impact on security in Asia, for example. Even France and the UK together could not pacify Libya: US assets were required to undertake the air campaign in 2011, and EU means would have been required to stabilize the country afterwards. In the end therefore, even the UK is but an off-shore Belgium, as I heard an American academic put it, to the consternation of his British co-panellists: it does not have much more freedom to pursue grand strategy alone than my own country.

Most do not have a strategy, and those that do do not have the means to implement it: is not the logical conclusion to pool both the strategic reflection and the means at the EU level?

That is not what the Member States did, however, at least not quite immediately. The European Union came into being in November 1993, when the Treaty of Maastricht entered into force and the preceding European Economic Community (EEC) was absorbed into a more overtly political Union, with the aspiration to pursue a Common Foreign and Security Policy (CFSP). In 1999 a politico-military arm was added to the CFSP, equipping the EU to undertake autonomous military operations and civilian missions: originally the European Security and Defence Policy (ESDP), it is now known as the Common Security and Defence Policy (CSDP). The ESS was only adopted fully ten years later however. Even the fact that the creation of the ESDP made the use of force possible under the EU flag did not prompt a debate on strategy. Instead, Member States purposely avoided any strategic debate, for the good reason that they knew very well that it would be impossible to agree because of their widely different views on the degree of autonomy of EU policy *vis-à-vis* the capitals themselves and *vis-à-vis* the US. That did not halt progress in other dimensions of foreign and security policy: Member States often pragmatically agree to disagree on one aspect, which allows them to take the issues forward on which they do agree. Thus the institutions of CFSP and CSDP were created and important foreign policy initiatives launched, such as the Euro-Mediterranean Partnership (1995) with Europe's southern neighbours.

Indeed, the absence of a formal strategy does not necessarily mean that all action is un-strategic. During the first decade of the CFSP, an implicit "European way" of doing things emerged from the practice of EU foreign policy-making, characterized by cooperation with partner countries, conflict prevention, and a broad approach through aid, trade and diplomacy. The origins of this approach go back very far, for it has roots in the external relations of the EEC. Although it had no formal competence in foreign policy, the Community developed dense trade relations across the globe and built up a network of delegations more encompassing than the network of embassies of any of its Member States. This implicit concept of strategy – for one cannot call it a fully-fledged strategy – steered the development of EU partnerships and long-term policies such as development. It proved entirely insufficient when the EU was confronted with crisis. It was the failure of the EU to comprehensively address the war in Bosnia and Herzegovina in the early 1990s and again in Kosovo in 1999 that drove the institutional development of the CFSP and the CSDP. Even perfect institutions will not deliver though if there is no strategy for them to operate on.

That insight finally came to the Member States of the EU in 2003. That year the US invasion of Iraq created a deep divide within Europe, between those who wanted to stand by their most important ally no matter what, and those who felt that even an ally cannot be followed when it so clearly violates one's own principles and, as would turn out all too soon, acts against one's interests. British Prime Minister Tony Blair seemed to have been captivated entirely by the regime-changing interventionism of the neo-conservatives advising US President George W. Bush, to the extent even of copying his messianic rhetoric. Belgian Prime Minister Guy Verhofstadt hosted a summit of Belgium, France, Germany and Luxembourg, all vehemently opposed to launching a war on flimsy evidence of the existence of weapons of mass destruction (WMD) in Iraq (the alternative motivation, to bring democracy, was put forward only post factum, when the Bush administration had to concede that no WMD were to be found). But whatever Europeans thought, it did not matter. This was the great lesson of the Iraq crisis (apart from the fact that one cannot change a regime, let alone a society, at gunpoint): when Europe is divided, it has no influence. Neither side in the European debate had any impact on American decision-making whatsoever. From this originated the unexpected drive to finally organize a formal strategic debate in the EU and to produce a strategic document. EU Member States had to heal the wounds which the at times very emotional debate about Iraq had left. Codifying the consensus on elements of strategy where it existed was at the same time to project an image of unity to the outside world again. Finally, this was a form of messaging to the US (Biscop and Andersson, 2008). Those who had supported the US-led invasion of Iraq wanted to signal to the Americans that Europe was still an ally and that it cared about the same threats and challenges as the US. Those who had opposed the invasion wanted to make it clear that caring about the same threats and challenges does not imply addressing them in the same way.

This window of opportunity was not wasted. Javier Solana, then the High Representative, was tasked with producing a first draft, which a small team around him elaborated and which he then proposed to the Heads of State and Government meeting at the European Council in June. Then the EU introduced an interesting innovation in the drafting process. Instead of discussing points and commas, working one's way up through the hierarchy of CFSP bodies, which is the normal procedure for the elaboration of official EU foreign policy texts, Solana had three seminars organized, where the same officials could give their input on the draft, but alongside representatives from national parliaments, from key allies and partners, and from academia and civil society. Having participated myself, I can testify that as an academic one really felt to be part of the debate. Perhaps only because they happened to echo what important capitals felt, but many comments and suggestions made at the seminars did find their way into the final document. In some corners Solana was criticized for circumventing formal procedure, but his approach created a much greater sense of ownership and produced a text that, unlike most EU documents, is short and free of jargon, and actually readable. His method was later copied by NATO, when it revised its strategic concept in 2010. The final document was formally adopted by the European Council as the European Security Strategy in December 2003. A strategy was born.

The Positive Strength of European Strategy

If "know thyself" is the first rule of strategy-making, then the first question when writing a European strategy is: what is Europe? The answer was put as perceptively as concisely by the great British historian Tony Judt (2005, p. 793), who at the end of his magisterial *Postwar* concluded: it is the "European Social Model".

Through a combination of democracy, capitalism – or the free market, if capitalism sounds too aggressive – and government intervention at the European and at the national level, Europeans have constructed a very distinctive model of society. Being distinctive is not an objective in its own right – North Korea is very distinctive too but that does not make it a model to emulate – but Europe really is distinguished by its egalitarian aspiration, what Judt (2005, p. 793) calls "a sense … of the balance of social rights, civic solidarity and collective responsibility … a social consensus … regarded by many citizens a formally binding". What is more, the European social model really works: Europe is the most equal continent on the planet, providing the greatest security, freedom, and prosperity to the greatest number of citizens. Security: every citizen has to be kept free from harm. Freedom: every citizen needs to participate in democratic decision-making (which is a duty as much as a right), has to have his human rights respected, and has to be equally treated before the law. But prosperity as well: every citizen has a right to a fair share of the wealth that his society produces; not an equal share, but a just one. Security, freedom and prosperity are the three core public goods to which every citizen is entitled. They are inextricably related: unless one is provided with all three, one cannot enjoy any single one of them. It is no good being rich if one risks getting shot at the moment one steps outside one's door; vice versa it is little consolation that one's country is free from any military threat if one is dying of hunger. Providing these public goods is the responsibility of government, at all levels, from local through regional and national government up to the EU level.

Things are far from perfect (every single European living below the poverty line is one too many), and there are many differences in how the social model is organized between one Member State and another. Care should be taken that new Member States in Eastern Europe move in the same direction rather than diluting the model, while reforming and deepening it in countries like the original six that founded the EEC. But the aspiration is real and shared. In 2009, the Member States even formally codified it in the Lisbon Treaty, which amended Article 2 of the Treaty on European Union and added equality and solidarity to the list of values on which European integration is based:

> The Union is founded on the values of respect for human dignity, freedom, democracy, equality, the rule of law and respect for human rights, including the rights of persons belonging to minorities. These values are common to the Member States in a society in which pluralism, non-discrimination, tolerance, justice, solidarity and equality between men and women prevail.

What many have forgotten is that the construction of this social model was, and remains, an inherent part of the European project. Everybody is familiar with the founding myth of the EU: after the end of the World War II, in order to prevent for ever more that another world war would start in Europe, the founding fathers, in their great foresight and wisdom, launched upon a path of integration between states that would make war between them a practical impossibility. The mantra has been repeated so often that we have become bored with it, which obscures the fact that the plan has worked. In view of the history of Europe, assuring peace between the members of the EEC/EU is an incredible success.

But: this is only half of the story. At the same time as they started the process of European integration, the countries of (western) Europe made a quantum leap in the establishment of the comprehensive welfare state. For a reason: they had learned that without the social buffer of the welfare state, democracy could not cope with severe economic crisis and the resulting political upheaval. In the 1930s, as a result, in the majority of European countries democracy had collapsed and given way to various forms of authoritarianism and fascism, which inevitably led to war. Already during the war statesmen began to devise a post-war social model that sought to prevent the lure of the strong man solution from threatening democracy ever again. The Beveridge Report, for example, which formed the basis for the British welfare state, dates from 1942. In the Belgian case, the decrees on social security were elaborated by the government in exile in London and implemented immediately upon its return to Brussels in the second half of 1944, even before the country had been liberated in its entirety. For the founding fathers, the social model was an inherent part of their peace project. It is not a luxury product, something that is nice to have when things are going well and can easily be discarded as ballast when things are going badly; on the contrary, the worse things get, the more important the social buffer is. It is precisely in times of crisis that one has to invest in it. At the time building the welfare state was of course a national undertaking. Today however, when we have a single market and, for most Member States, a currency union, a banking union, and common budgetary rules enforced by the European Commission, maintaining the social model increasingly requires that some aspects at least are incorporated into this common European system of governance. Which is exactly what Commissioner Marianne Thyssen (2015) proposed in June 2015, pleading for minimum unemployment benefits, a minimum income, and access to child care and to basic health care in all Member States.

The strength of the ESS is that it takes this very same egalitarian aspiration and turns it into a positive, even optimist narrative for European foreign and security policy. "A secure Europe in a better world": the subtitle of the ESS says it all. The aim is to secure Europe; the best way of making that happen is to make the world a better place: isn't that a good start? This is not a strategy against somebody else, but a strategy aimed at realizing a positive agenda. The core of this philosophy is neatly captured in just two sentences, which express the essence of EU strategy:

> The best protection for our security is a world of well-governed democratic states. Spreading good governance, supporting social and political reform, dealing with corruption and abuse of power, establishing the rule of law and protecting human rights are the best means of strengthening the international order (European Council, 2003).

In other words, the key to security are effective states that provide for the security, freedom and prosperity of their own citizens. Only where governments treat their citizens equally are lasting peace and stability possible. Empirical research shows that even countries that are poorer but where citizens are more equal will be more stable, healthier societies, than richer but less equal countries (Krugman, 2012; Stiglitz, 2012; Wilkinson and Pickett, 2009). Where governments do not provide for their citizens however, tensions will arise, instability, repression and conflict will follow; citizens will eventually revolt, and regimes will either implode, relatively peacefully (think of the Soviet Union in 1991 or Tunisia in 2011), or explode, with a lot of violence (as is happening all around Europe today). Therefore, put less diplomatically: the more the rest of the world becomes like Europe, the better for everybody. The better for Europe, for there will be less ground for mass migration to Europe (always a concern of European governments), less interruption of trade, and less risk of conflict spilling over to its territory. But the better also for citizens in the rest of the world, for they will enjoy more security, freedom and prosperity.

That does not mean however that the EU should simply be trying to export its own social model in all its intricate detail to the rest of the world. Not only would that be all too paternalistic or neo-imperialist, more importantly, it just would not work. Circumstances around the world are too different for a one-size-fits-all model. What Europe should try to promote is the core values: the egalitarian aspiration, the sense that government is responsible for the common weal, for the *res publica* – and not just for the wellbeing of the ruling elite. Europeans should abandon the idea that they know better how to govern other countries than the citizens of those countries themselves, but they can legitimately advertise the results that they have achieved in Europe. There are probably many ways of achieving the same result, and it is the result, as well as the sincere commitment to at least attempt it, that counts.

It is legitimate to stimulate governments outside Europe to aspire to the same result – better and more equal provision of security, freedom and prosperity – because in many cases that is what their own citizens are already demanding, loudly and clearly. The brave people who went out into the streets in Tunisia in 2011, whose actions would bring down the authoritarian regime of Ben Ali and trigger the Arab Spring, demonstrated because they wanted exactly that: a government that protects their security, respects their human rights, gives them a say in decision-making, and tries to make the economy work for everybody. These Tunisian demonstrators were not different from Belgian workers striking, and getting shot at, for the right to vote in the 1880s, Polish trade unionists resisting dictatorship in the 1980s, or Chinese citizens denouncing corruption today.

Finally, it is not just legitimate for European foreign policy to embody the same values on which its domestic social model is based – it is a moral duty. No polity can be called truly democratic unless it is democratic in all of its actions. One could never imagine that for the sake of expediency the EU or any Member State government would suspend the rule of law or respect for human rights when dealing with, say, the Common Agricultural Policy or regulation of the telecommunications sector. It should be as unimaginable to do so in foreign and security policy. This goes against the sense of Realpolitik, which has led many to advocate, like former senior EU foreign policy official Sir Robert Cooper (2004, p. 62), that when one operates in the jungle, one must abide by the laws of the jungle. That assumes though that the jungle cannot be cultivated. If one never tries, it never will be, for sure. If Europe gives up on its own values, its foreign policy would perpetuate the very challenges that it tries to address: war, authoritarianism, and inequality.

The more Europe is perceived to bring the values that it propagates into practice, not just in its foreign policy but even more so domestically, the more legitimacy it gains with citizens of other countries. To offer some anecdotal evidence: when teaching my annual class on EU foreign policy at the People's University in Beijing, it is useless trying to convince the Chinese students that Europe is a great power. That they find a laughable proposition (if one evolution is evident since I started teaching there in 2006, it is the increased self-confidence of the students, and rightfully so). But they do feel that European governments sincerely care about their citizens' wellbeing and try to address their grievances, and that in many ways their own government does not (as daily concerns about air pollution and food safety, for example, make clear). Many Europeans who are in the habit of complaining about their governments may feel that this perception is exaggerated, but it reveals a crucial truth: the biggest source of Europe's influence is neither its soldiers nor even its trade, but the success of the way it does things internally. It is interesting to see that in its latest National Security Strategy even the US makes a (feeble) attempt to advertise its "competitive edge and leadership in … healthcare (The White House, 2015, p. 3), though few will regard "Obama-care" and the infighting about it as a source of strength.

The implication for Europe is evident: a strategy founded on promoting our values and the results of our social model outside the EU cannot be credible if we no longer adhere to it ourselves – that would kick the feet from under the strategic narrative. Unfortunately this is exactly what the EU and several Member States began to do when the financial and economic crisis hit Europe.

That the crisis did not bode well for EU foreign policy was self-evident (Youngs, 2014). In times of austerity, first, there simply is less money available for external action. Foreign policy in the narrow sense, or diplomacy, may not seem such a costly policy area, but as we shall see the EU precisely adopts a broad, holistic approach that comprises partnership, investment and development – which does cost money. Secondly, there was limited bandwidth available for foreign policy. As the EU Heads of State and Government struggled to address the Eurozone crisis, devoting summit after summit to this natural priority, foreign policy inevitably lost out. Faced with the fact that the Eurozone as it existed did not work, Member States could do one of two things: they could abandon the Euro, or they could save the Eurozone by deepening financial and economic integration. The fundamental choice for the latter option has been made, and the trend therefore remains ever closer union. But, thirdly, the painful and drawn-out decision-making process created the image of a weak Union, paralysed by dissent and unable to take resolute action. And it ain't over yet … Could anyone imagine that it would be seriously considered to kick a state out of the United States? Yet this is what many in the EU seem to steer at when it comes to Greece. All of this inevitably undermines the credibility of any foreign policy initiative which the EU might want to undertake.

But the Eurozone crisis also affected EU foreign policy at a less evident but actually much more fundamental level, because the way in which it was initially addressed was basically at odds with the values underpinning both EU foreign policy and the EU as such. For far too long, how to save the Euro was presented as a technocratic issue, devoid of political or ideological choices. The medicine was known, it was just a matter of convincing the unwilling patient to swallow it. Certainly the purpose could not be doubted: the Euro had to be saved. But not as an end in itself. The Euro is a political project, of course, and a symbol of European integration, but first of all it is but a means – a means to enhance the security, freedom and prosperity of European citizens. If the Euro were to be saved in such a manner that the prosperity and equality of European citizens were destroyed, the end result would be extremely dangerous for the European project as such. For the social consensus that Judt mentioned would be broken and citizens would no longer feel committed to the Union and the governments that did not respect it. There was a reason why Judt (2010) entitled his next book *Ill Fares the Land*. Great internal instability would be the result – hardly a base for decisive external action. Saving the Euro the wrong way would be as bad for the EU as not saving it at all.

Fortunately, it has dawned on (most of) Europe's leaders that jobs and growth are more likely to save the Union than austerity. Under its President Jean-Claude Juncker this is the direction which the European Commission has decided to take. Yet obsessed with austerity the EU and many governments had already gone very far. The eight foreign ministers of the Future of Europe Group (2012) deplored the dwindling of the "feeling of solidarity and sense of belonging in Europe" as a result of the crisis. Restoring it will be a work of many years.

The Inconsistency in Implementing European Strategy

By adopting the ESS, the Heads of State and Government provided the formal underpinning of the European way of doing foreign policy that was already emerging through the practice of EU external action, and gave it a conceptual basis. Rather than a radical new departure, the ESS thus marks the codification and consolidation of a specific European approach.

This approach, first of all, clearly puts the emphasis on prevention. By attempting to improve the provision of public goods, EU foreign policy seeks to address the root causes of tensions, disputes and conflicts. If successful, conflict should be avoided altogether. Unfortunately, there will always be cases when prevention will fail and the choice will be to act militarily or not to act at all, but the aspiration is clear. Secondly, the approach is comprehensive or holistic: because security, freedom and prosperity are interrelated, every external action undertaken addresses all three dimensions simultaneously, integrating all available EU instruments, from aid and trade to diplomacy and the military. Unidimensional interventions may combat the symptoms of a problem, but will not produce lasting effect, and risk having negative side effects. The classic example is the US invasion of Iraq: military victory was quickly gained, but for lack of a political and economic strategy to accompany it, it only produced another (civil) war. But Europeans seemed not to have absorbed that lesson and made exactly the same mistake when, with US support, they intervened in Libya in 2011. As a result, no stable new regime has yet emerged, and furthermore many combatants were pushed into Mali, necessitating another military intervention soon afterwards. Finally, the EU approach is multilateral: the aim is to influence other governments, not to subjugate them, hence an emphasis on dialogue and partnership, notably with the UN and the global multilateral agencies, with regional organizations, and with the great powers (because they are the great powers and therefore cannot be ignored).

All of this may seem like motherhood and apple pie: who could possibly be against it? But formally adopting this approach in the wake of a National Security Strategy (The White House, 2002) in which the US reserved the right to unilateral pre-emptive military intervention ("before a threat is fully formed", as President Bush's cover letter stated), this was a very conscious choice to do things differently. The strategy plays out at two levels. In the EU's own neighbourhood, it seeks to take the lead itself and establish a ring of well-governed countries around it. At the global level, Europe opts for the indirect approach: promoting cooperation in regional and other multilateral frameworks, thus pulling states into what the EU calls "effective multilateralism". Multilateralism can be deemed effective if it increases security, freedom and prosperity. This is grand strategy, a single framework for all of EU external action, across the complex EU institutional machinery, from the European Commission (development, trade, enlargement, humanitarian aid) to the European External Action Service (diplomacy and defence).

What everybody wants to know is, of course: does this strategy work?

It certainly works as a narrative. At the time, many expected that once adopted, the ESS would be quickly forgotten, locked into some drawer and the key given to NATO. The opposite has happened: to this day EU foreign policy decisions refer to the ESS as the overall framework, and EU and national officials continue to refer to it when explaining Europe's role in the world, because it expresses it so neatly and concisely. That is important, for in a disparate actor such as the EU, with 28 Member States each with its own strategic culture, commonality must be stressed time and again. To that end, for example, almost every course organized by the EU's European Security and Defence College (ESDC) for national and EU diplomats, military and others who will work on EU foreign policy starts with a lecture on the ESS. I know, for I am usually the one giving it.

But the most important question is of course whether having a strategy drives a proactive EU foreign policy, and helps the EU make the right decisions in moments of crisis? Here the picture is more mixed, for the simple reason that the ESS is not a complete strategy at all. In the ESS, the EU is very clear about its values, which it translates into very specific ways: Europe wants to tackle things in a preventive, comprehensive and multilateral way. The strategy has little to say however about either the means, apart from a general recognition that in the military field especially more is required, or, even more importantly, the objectives. The choice to prioritize assuming leadership in stabilizing Europe's own neighbourhood is an important one; opting for a more indirect approach at the global level is the logical corollary, for one cannot prioritize everything at once. In the ESS itself, neither broad objective is detailed into more specific priorities however that could drive day-to-day decision-making. Furthermore, Member States have not used the ESS either as a basis to generate (and continuously and systematically debate and review) specific common objectives on which to focus EU foreign policy, complementing their national foreign policies. The ESS, in conclusion, codifies *how* to do things – but it does not really tell Europe *what* to do first.

None of this has stopped the EU from being active – far from it – but (as sketched in the prologue) it is so mainly in a programmatic and a reactive way. A minimal part of the budget may be shifted from one column to the other, but too often Europe has a long-term policy because it had the same policy last year, without really assessing whether the objectives are being reached or are even still valid (effectiveness), and how much any achievements have cost (efficiency). In the absence of clear objectives, the various strands of EU engagement (aid, trade, diplomacy, defence) tend to be stove-piped: each part of the machinery does its thing without too much coordination with the other, even when operating in the same country or on the same issue. Coordination with Member State initiatives is often limited too, although in most cases the critical mass necessary to shape developments can be achieved only if the EU and the Member States pool their efforts. Consequently, results are sub-optimal and short-lived. On short-term issues and in crisis situations, things are even worse. Conclusion: effective prevention remains difficult, and to what it has not been able to prevent, the EU tends to react late. Furthermore, the allocation of the means bears little relation to any prioritization of objectives.

All of this is contrary to the other great powers, especially the US, China and Russia, which usually have a much clearer idea of what their interests and their objectives are. This does not necessarily always make them successful, but it does mean that they can act much more purposively than Europeans, who often do not know what they want, or whether they want anything at all, or have 28 different ideas. To borrow an expression from Jo Coelmont: while the other great powers (or should that simply be: the great powers) are playing chess, the EU is playing ping-pong (Biscop and Coelmont, 2012, p. 124). That does not require much thinking ahead. The image of the EU that results from this state of affairs is easily tested: ask anyone working on, for or with the EU whether he or she sees Europe (in all meanings of the term) as a game-changer in international politics today, or even simply as a strategic actor, and the response will be hesitation at best; many will simply answer no. Nobody would hesitate for a second were the same question asked about the US or China.

The EU's major engagement in the Democratic Republic of the Congo can serve to illustrate that activity is no substitute for strategy. The EU and the Member States are the number one donor; Europe keeps the Congo on the agenda of the international community when necessary, notably in the Security Council; the EU has twice intervened military under its own flag (in 2003 and 2006); and it has two civilian missions ongoing to assist with the reform of the police and the armed forces. But does anybody think that the future of the Congo is determined in Europe? In fact, what does Europe seek to achieve that merits, and gives a joint purpose to, all this activity? If the country is a priority, then why does Europe not contribute to the UN force stationed there permanently since 2000? If not, then why bother at all? Absent clear objectives and more than token ownership by Member States, no amount of activity will produce strategic effect. If one does not know what one's objective is, the chance of achieving it is small.

Fortunately, there increasingly are good examples of strategic engagement as well.

From launching a naval operation, Atalanta, to combat Somali piracy in 2008, the EU gradually evolved towards a comprehensive strategy for the Horn of Africa as a whole, including training the Somali armed forces, capacity-building in all the littoral states, and development aid. Subsequently the EU formalized this truly comprehensive approach into a document (Council of the EU, 2011a). The piracy problem has been brought under control, but will resurface the moment the foreign navies leave the area, as long as Somalia is not fully stabilized. Europe and the international community will have to remain committed for a long time to come therefore. Nevertheless, though Somalia has been in turmoil since the early 1990s, the country does now finally seem to be on a slow road to stability.

Informed by its engagement in the Horn of Africa, the EU then conceived a regional strategy for the Sahel from the start (Council of the EU, 2011b). Within this framework it took to the initiative on Mali, envisaging a political roadmap towards a legitimate national government for the divided country and towards a consensus with the Touareg population, and planning a training mission to enable the Mali armed forces to deal with the security situation in the north of the country, which had deteriorated drastically by the fall-out of the Libyan crisis. Unfortunately, when in January 2013 jihadist militias, strengthened by an influx of combatants who had fled Libya, suddenly seemed poised to take the capital, which would have rendered this EU strategy obsolete, the EU as such proved unable to respond. A rapid French military intervention, with the support of individual European countries, had to stabilize the situation before the EU military training mission could be deployed. In Niger as well, the EU is on the ground, with a civilian advisory mission.

In the negotiations about the nuclear capacity of Iran, the EU (represented by Britain, France and Germany plus the High Representative) has played a vital role for many years, keeping talks going while the US, during the Bush administration, was not interested, until finally President Barack Obama brought the US back to the negotiating table. The framework agreement that was finally reached in Lausanne on 2 April 2015 could be the start of a normalization of relations with Iran, which in turn, as we shall see in Chapter 2, is of great importance to any attempt to stabilize the Middle East and the Gulf. Chapter 2 will also explain how in dealing with Russia in the context of the Ukraine crisis, the EU is playing the leading role in forging a diplomatic solution, putting Moscow under pressure by the adoption of a hard-hitting sanctions regime.

What all these examples have in common is that European *interests* are quite obviously at stake: seaborne trade in the Horn, energy as well as fear of general instability and terrorism in the Sahel, the survival of the nuclear non-proliferation regime, the security of Europe's eastern borders. As seen in the prologue, the EU is gradually getting past the times when many officials regarded interests as a notion that does not or should not apply to the EU, considering the pursuit of interests to run contrary to their idealized view of an altruistic EU foreign policy. Another notion that needs to be put to rest is that differences between the national interests of the Member States render collective action impossible. Of course, geography and history generate differences in the focus of national foreign policies. Belgium will show more interest in the Congo than Poland, and Poland will care more about Belarus than Portugal. But this should not obscure the fact that objectively all Member States, because they constitute an integrated economy with a distinctive social model, have shared *vital* interests. When one tries to draw up the list of vital interests, those that guarantee the very survival of European society, one ends up with the same result for each country, and thus for the EU as a whole, which can be summarized in seven points:

1. Preventing direct military threats against Europe's territory from materializing: such threats may appear unlikely today, but that does not mean this will always be the case.
2. Keeping open all lines of interaction with the world, notably sea lanes and cyberspace: as a global trade power, any interruption of the global marketplace immediately damages the European economy.
3. Assuring the supply of energy and other natural resources that society and the economy need.
4. Managing migration in an ethically acceptable way: on the one hand migration is necessary in order to maintain a viable work force, yet on the other hand the social model might not be able to cope with a surplus of migration.
5. Mitigating the impact of climate change in order to limit the multiplier effect on security threats and, of course, to save the planet.
6. Upholding the core of international law, notably the interdiction of the use of force in the UN Charter and the Universal Declaration of Human Rights: the more the rules are respected, the better for international stability.
7. Preserving the autonomy of decision-making by preventing undue dependence on any foreign power: Europe should make its own decisions and not have decisions taken for it in Moscow or Beijing, or Washington for that matter.

Europe need not be timid in defending these interests. That is the point of policy-making: if one has no interests in an issue, one will not allocate means to it. But its interests would be well served by continuing to defend them in a way that does not harm the legitimate interests of others – that is the point of the "European way" of foreign policy. What is more, no Member State can defend these vital interests on its own any longer. In their 2010 Lancaster House Agreement on defence cooperation, the UK and France declared that they cannot imagine any situation in which the vital interests of one party are threatened and not those of the other. Surely if even Paris and London have come to this conclusion, so must the other Europeans. There is a positive trend, for in spite of the differences in focus, and though it does not yet translate in effective contributions in all theatres, all 28 capitals have recognized that stability on Europe's eastern and southern borders is equally important to the security of them all.

The positive examples of EU engagement show that the more directly vital interests are at stake, the more EU Member States are willing to act collectively through the Union. Any decision is always preceded by difficult debates – it would be surprising if it would not, when 28 states have to find consensus. What is typical for the EU is that these debates rarely remain secret, contrary to actors like the US and China, where the internal debate is often as vigorous but usually much less visible. A debating EU does not equal a divided EU though: what counts are the decisions that ultimately are taken. These examples further show that the EU is learning by doing. Europe has all the instruments and it still has substantial means, but putting them to use in an integrated way and making the preventive, comprehensive and multilateral foreign policy work remains a challenge. Some very good regional strategies have been elaborated, like those for the Horn and the Sahel (and the EU also has functional strategies, on terrorism, proliferation, etc.), but there is no clear mechanism to arbitrate between them. Without an encompassing grand strategy in which to anchor the regional strategies, conflicts will inevitably arise between them, perfect though each in itself may be. How for example to reconcile the emphasis on security cooperation with Algeria in the Sahel strategy, with the same country's imperviousness to EU human rights objectives under the Neighbourhood Policy? Without an up-to-date grand strategy, furthermore, the EU cannot sensibly react to events such as the US pivot and the financial crisis that simply affect everything, and hence may require a reprioritization and reallocation of means between regional strategies.

The most important conclusion from this assessment of the practice of EU strategy is this. If they want to, Europeans can act strategically through the EU and collectively safeguard their national interests – but they do not always want to. The national outlook remains predominant. If a crisis happens in Syria or Ukraine, most if not all in the Belgian foreign ministry will ask "What will the EU do?", which means "What will Belgium, through the EU, do?" But as long as those in the Foreign Office, the Quai d'Orsay and the Auswärtiges Amt ask "What will Britain, France or Germany do?", the EU as such is always likely not to do very much. Although most Member States individually would be utterly unable to have any impact on them, and in many cases would not even have a position, Europeans do not consistently consider the big issues of the day together, in order to decide together what has to be done, how, and with which means. And can a strategic actor that does not engage consistently when its interests are at stake really be considered a strategic actor at all?

Taking European Strategy-Making Forward

The implication is not that collective EU foreign policy and the method that the ESS prescribes for it must be discarded. Quite the opposite: collective action increasingly becomes the only option to defend the interests of the states of Europe on the big issues that they are facing today. What they need to do is to have a strategic debate and decide what the big issues are that they *all* care about, and set out a programme of action, to increase the consistency of European strategic engagement.

As much was attempted in 2008, actually, at the instigation of France and Sweden primarily, when the European Council tasked Solana not with writing a new strategy, as many had expected and kept hoping for, but to assess the implementation of the existing ESS. More the Member States could not agree on. The exercise was ill-timed however, as the EU was in the midst of the ratification process of the Lisbon Treaty, and no capital wanted to be seen to pre-empt ratification, which greatly hindered a thorough debate. Seminars were again organized involving academics, NGOs and third countries, four this time, but having participated in all of them my impression was that only the academics were really interested. In the end the European Council (2008) adopted a soon forgotten implementation report on the ESS – long in words but meagre in substance. Its most important effect was a negative one: it created a reluctance to reopen the formal EU strategic debate. Within the EU institutions, many of the officials involved preferred to avoid another potentially futile exercise. Catherine Ashton, who succeeded Solana as High Representative in 2009, expressed her lack of interest in strategy on many occasions. The "big three", Britain, France and Germany, lost their interest as well (though for Paris and London in particular it does appear rather contradictory to engage in very elaborate national strategic processes and then assume that at the much more complex EU level one can do without). The only Member States that continued to push for a strategic review were sort of the "middle powers": Sweden, Finland, Poland, Italy, Spain – countries that have a view about the world but have also realized that they can only implement it collectively through the EU. That coalition proved insufficiently grand to tip the balance however and the deadlock remained. All they could achieve was to launch an informal track, tasking a consortium of think-tanks to produce a report on a "European Global Strategy" in an attempt to keep the debate alive (UI, PISM, IAI and Elcano, 2013).

This reluctance shows how little the EU and the Member States were still at ease at the time with questions of strategy and geopolitics. The many arguments that were raised against a European strategic review are easily refuted, actually. True, a serious strategic debate would lay bare the differences between Member States, but it is precisely because they are divided and therefore collectively inactive on several crucial issues that a debate is necessary. If one were to debate only what one already agrees upon, that would quickly become very boring. Many capitals advocated focusing on the consolidation of the newly-established (from 2009) European External Action Service. That was a priority, of course, but the EEAS is but a means, which can only be meaningful if it serves clear ends. The financial means were (and are) under pressure, but as stated in the preface already, that renders strategy and prioritization even more important. Many feared that a new strategy could never be as good as the original ESS. That is a compliment to Solana and his team, but as long as one keeps the number of drafters below the number of pages, it is certainly possible to produce an equally concise, readable and substantial text. Far too often indeed the debate between Member States has focussed on form and process (Does the EU need a new ESS-type document and who will draft it?) rather than on substance (What should EU strategy be?). Had half the time spent on debating the former been spent on the latter, a new strategy would have been adopted a long time ago. In comparison, the US has updated its National Security Strategy (upon the 2002 iteration of which the ESS closely followed) thrice in the same time frame, in 2006, 2010 and 2015, and NATO adopted a new strategic concept in 2010 as well.

Slowly but surely, things are changing. First, Member States discovered the importance of comprehensive regional strategies, such as those for the Sahel and the Horn. Then, the Arab Spring and the resulting wars and upheaval, followed by the Ukraine crisis, rendered obsolete many existing EU policies, including regional strategies like the Eastern Partnership and the Union for the Mediterranean. Nobody could pretend that the EU could carry on as if nothing had happened. In December 2013 therefore the Heads of State and Government gave a tasking to the High Representative: "in close cooperation with the Commission", she was "to assess the impact of changes in the global environment, and to report to the Council in the course of 2015 on the challenges and opportunities arising for the Union, following consultations with the Member States" (European Council, 2013). This was rather cryptic language (only the initiated understood that it meant "do something about strategy"), highlighting that even now many Member States saw the strategic debate as inevitable rather than desirable. In any case, when Mogherini took over the reins from Ashton in 2014 she immediately stressed the importance of a real strategic review.

How to go about it, not just now, but in the future as well?
The starting point – know thyself – is the acknowledgement that the core of what Europe is, how Europe has brought universal values into practice, is its social model; preserving and even deepening this must be seen as the fundamental purpose of the Union and its Member States. For that to be possible, the seven vital interests outlined above have to be safeguarded. The next step then is to analyse the world around Europe. We are living in a multipolar and interdependent world. There are more powers with global range, who are competing for scarce resources. At the same time their economies are deeply interwoven and they are facing complex global challenges such as climate change that neither can solve alone. This does not guarantee that the great powers will cooperate, but it does increase the chance that they might cooperate and attempt to manage tensions peacefully. In this "interpolar" world, the term coined by Giovanni Grevi (2009), the EU's preventive, comprehensive and multilateral way of doing foreign policy remains as valid as ever, in order to stimulate the other powers to work through the multilateral institutions, on a comprehensive range of issues, wherever their interests coincide, so as to avoid tension and conflict.

EU strategy does not have to start from a blank page therefore, but would do best to reconfirm the "how to" that the ESS already defined. That is not enough though; another statement of principle, merely paraphrasing the existing ESS, would not have much added value. Though the narrative should always remain short and sharp, and positively-framed, it should also be ambitious, starting from the threats but then focusing on what the EU wants to achieve. A merely threat-based agenda will produce a reactive, defensive or even antagonistic foreign policy; a positive agenda on the other hand will stimulate initiative, transparency and partnership in dealing with the challenges that Europe does face. The crux of a strategic review is to identify, on the basis of a geopolitical analysis of the regional and global environment, what the most important threats and challenges are to Europe's vital interests, and to define priority objectives (the "what") to which end the preventive, comprehensive and multilateral method must be applied.

EU strategy should not try to say a little something about everything therefore. Of course EU foreign policy actions have to, and do, cover an incredibly broad range of issues and countries, from organized crime in Columbia to nuclear safety in Japan. But the function of strategy is to fix the priorities among those. Similarly, the aim is not to compile a long and equally useless list of all the national priorities of all the Member States. The point of EU foreign policy is not to replace Member States' national policies, but to complement them where necessary. EU strategy should prioritize those foreign policy issues that (1) all Member States regard as priorities because their shared vital interests are most directly at stake and that (2) are so challenging that no Member State can deal with them alone. These are the types of issues on which EU foreign policy will bring the greatest added value as compared to what the Member States can do. This is where the EU can and must prove that it is better at defending Member States' interests than the Member States themselves.

The resulting three, four or five priorities have to be seen as a programme for *action*, now. A strategic actor requires a strategy: it needs to know who it is and what it wants; it needs the economic means to pursue its strategy; but probably most important of all, it needs the will to act upon it. In the words of the great British strategic thinker Colin Gray:

> Just because a government drafts a document which proclaims the existence of a grand strategy, or a 'comprehensive approach', there is no guarantee that the baronies of officialdom will behave cohesively, coherently, and comprehensively. Strategy, grand or military, is never self-executing. (2010, p. 28)

The purpose is not to enshrine a set of EU priorities that remain valid for evermore, to be carved into the walls of the EEAS building on the Schuman Roundabout in Brussels. That would be the opposite of strategy, for "as soon as it allows the expectations of theory to obscure its vision of what is really happening, then strategy is not only no longer helpful, it is positively pernicious" (Strachan, 2013, p. 103). What is required is suppleness in systematically reassessing the importance of Europe's interests and the threats and challenges facing it, evaluating past actions, and reprioritizing objectives and the allocation of means accordingly, thus producing a strategy for collective EU action for the short to medium term. Just like a national foreign minister produces a policy statement at the start of each term of office, so the High Representative should organize an update of EU strategy at least at the beginning of each five-year term. Perhaps on some occasions the decision will be that not much has to be changed, but then at least it will be a conscious choice and not the result of avoiding the debate, as it has been since 2008. There is a risk that a five-yearly strategic review would become a ritualistic exercise without true importance. Certainly not all editions of the US National Security Strategy have been equally important. But a High Representative that is a politician will have an idea of where he or she wants to leave his or her mark. In the full knowledge that a large part of the job will naturally consist in reacting to events, he or she must set a proactive agenda and assess on which issues only Europeans together can and have to try and actively shape, rather than just undergo, events. In other words, a systematic strategic review would produce a mandate for the High Representative and the EU institutions for the next five years to take the initiative and to act.

Only when the substance is decided should the question of form be addressed. Ideally, each update of grand strategy would generate a document adopted by the European Council, every time replacing its predecessor (so at this stage it would replace the ESS). The document need not spell out everything though. On the one hand, every five-yearly strategic review must be understood as a tasking to revise specific regional and issue-based strategies. The grand strategy should define the level of ambition and provide overall substantial guidance, and give a tasking, deadline included, to take things forward to the relevant EU bodies. On the other hand, certain assumptions can remain implicit, hence the importance of the process as such. As Robert Hunter (2009, p. 80), a veteran of many strategic debates in NATO advises: "following the conclusion of the exercise, everyone has a better idea of where each ally stands, what the agenda ... is likely to be, and, in general, a set of overall aspirations ...". The process ideally involves outsiders (academics, NGOs, allies and partners), just as when the original ESS was drafted, to introduce some more creativity and daring. Process matters, but ultimately the outcome is what counts. Part of that outcome ought to be the enduring awareness in all capitals and in the EU institutions that strategy and grand strategy exist, and that choices have to be made at both levels, by each Member State where possible but collectively through the EU where necessary.

If this strategic exercise were undertaken today, at least four interconnected challenges stand out as priorities for collective EU action: (1) Europeans have to deal with the consequences of the "Arab Spring" and the Ukraine crisis in their broader neighbourhood; (2) they have to decide, now that the US is pivoting to Asia, which responsibilities they must assume themselves for security problems in that very neighbourhood as well as further afield; (3) Europeans have to increase their room of manoeuvre in foreign policy by reducing their energy dependence, notably *vis-à-vis* Russia; and (4) they have to reinvigorate multilateral cooperation on energy, climate change and other key issues, notably by making better use of their so-called strategic partnerships, in particular with the BRICS. The main challenges relating to all four priorities as well as the overall direction that a new EU strategy could provide on them will be sketched here. On the first two priorities I will also try to develop a more elaborate answer on how to implement those directions in the next two chapters, hoping that the reader will agree that two out of four is an acceptable score for the armchair strategist that I am.

The Broader Neighbourhood: Remember the Revolution

The aim of a strategic review is not only to redefine priorities but also to decide how these can best be addressed, through which instruments. Together, the nature of the objectives and of the instruments determine the type of actor, the type of power even, which Europe will be.

It may not fit in exactly with how most EU and Member State diplomats see themselves, but the 2003 ESS outlines an agenda for what in political science terms is called a revolutionary power: a power that seeks to change the existing order. To state, as the ESS does, that "the quality of international society depends on the quality of the governments that are its foundation" is to say in very couched yet clear enough terms that the EU does not think that that quality is now assured. To add, as we have seen, that "the best protection for our security is a world of well-governed democratic states" is nothing less than a call for regime-change across the globe, for there are alas far too few of these. The EU would of course like to see this happening gradually and smoothly, by stimulating governments to improve the provision of the core public goods of security, freedom and prosperity to their citizens, and certainly not by force of arms. Nonetheless this really is a revolutionary agenda. The European Neighbourhood Policy, which is one of two broad objectives identified in the 2003 ESS, was an attempt to bring it into practice on Europe's eastern and southern borders, through "positive conditionality": governments were offered greater access to the European market (for people, goods, services and capital) for every step they took towards more equal provision of security, freedom and prosperity for all their citizens.

Yet in contrast with the ambitious rhetoric of the ENP, in practice the EU more often behaves as a status quo power, which is happy with things as they are. The clearest symptom of this is Europe's addiction to partnership as a way of conducting international relations. It seems as if just about every country (except North Korea) has a formal partnership of some kind or other with the EU. In reality partnership cannot be the beginning of a diplomatic relationship but is its desired end-state. For effective partnership is only possible if there is sufficient consensus on foreign policy objectives and on what are acceptable ways of achieving them to enable systematic consultation and regular joint action. The EU has ten high-profile strategic partnerships: with NATO allies the United States and Canada, with the BRICS (Brazil, Russia, India, China, and South Africa), and with Japan, Mexico and, most recently, South Korea. But even with many of them that degree of consensus does not exist – unless one counts the fact that Russia's intervention in Ukraine has stimulated Europe's defence efforts as an emanation of the strategic partnership.

Rather than stimulating its "partners" to change (for why would they as they are on the list of the "good guys" already) the EU itself has become tainted by associating too uncritically with all kinds of unsavoury regimes. That is the consequence of something that happens rather too often in the EU: after a while it begins to mistake an aspirational notion in one of its policies for reality. Thus, Brussels ended up believing that all those which it had dubbed partners really were partners. Similarly it began to believe that the way the EU divides up the world between different policies and directorates really reflects reality on the ground, as if there is "a line in the sand" marking the borders of the ENP between, say, Libya and Mali. Europe's southern neighbourhood is a case in point. The EU gave up on its reform agenda and the promotion of the egalitarian aspiration in favour of a status quo policy and worked with every dictator that seemed to meet its concerns over terrorism, migration and energy supply. And then came the Arab Spring that toppled Europe's "partners" in Tunisia, Libya and Egypt... The east presents a mirror image: in Ukraine the EU pushed too fast too far, ignoring that the country was not ready for a Deep and Comprehensive Free Trade Agreement (DCFTA) and that its other neighbour, Russia, might have a not so benign reading of EU intentions. The resulting image is one of a blundering and reactive EU.

The easiest way to overcome this problem of double standards would be to simply give up on the high-flown rhetoric and pursue a status quo strategy in words as well as in deeds. That however is not an option for the EU. Why? Because, as we have seen, the notion that "the best protection for our security is a world of well-governed democratic states" remains absolutely true and is but the reflection of the EU itself. If EU foreign policy abandons its distinctiveness, this would be a disavowal of its own values – Europe would simply no longer be Europe. Europe would be but one international actor among others, and a weak one at that: an EU without its distinctive egalitarian project to promote would just be like the US, but without the latter's armed strength. The EU cannot and should not give up on its "revolutionary" agenda, but it must find better ways of achieving it.

Therefore a middle way has to be found – neither dreamy idealism nor unprincipled pragmatism. The revolutionary agenda has proved to be far too optimistic. If change does not emerge organically from within a country, it cannot be engineered from the outside. All attempts to do so have ended in disaster, witness Iraq and even Afghanistan. In such circumstances playing a reforming role is extremely difficult. However, a pure status quo policy, just working with the powers that be, has also proved to be harmful to Europe's interests. Regimes that do not provide for the security, freedom and prosperity of their citizens are inherently unstable and will eventually implode or explode – one cannot count on long-term cooperation therefore. When change does occur, driven internally, Europe has to be on the right side of history or it will find itself without legitimacy. An external actor can attempt to play a moderating role, aiming to curb excesses by exerting pressure via diplomatic channels, and in case of serious threats to EU interests or serious human rights violations, sanctions. Military intervention under the principle of the Responsibility to Protect is the ultimate emergency break in case of the gravest violations (genocide, ethnic cleansing, war crimes, and crimes against humanity), which only the Security Council can trigger. But these are emergency measures and not a basis for day-to-day policy.

The middle way could be an activist strategy of pragmatic idealism. To remain consistent with itself, Europe has to adhere to the long-term overall objective of "a world of well-governed democratic states", but in the knowledge that it will only be reached through mostly incremental steps.

Where, for the time being at least, the situation seems impervious to change Europe should at least not do anything that puts even more obstacles in the way of achieving "well-governed democratic states". In other words, if one does not see what can be done, at the very least do not do anything that clashes with one's own values. This is what George Kennan (quoted in Gaddis, 2011, p. 417) meant when he wrote: "Where purpose is dim and questionable, form comes into its own". Therefore a pure status quo policy of cooperation with the powers that be is not an option. This does not mean that the EU cannot cooperate at all with them. On the contrary, Brussels should seek to continuously engage all relevant actors in such countries, the opposition and civil society as well as the regime – but it cannot cooperate with any regime in ways that strengthen its authoritarian foundations. To put it very bluntly: rendition of terrorist suspects to be "interrogated" by the security services of an autocracy while preaching about human rights is not good for Europe's credibility. But the EU definitely ought to engage economically: trade and even more so investment leading to job creation are the best ways of permeating a society. And while Europeans invest around the world, it is notably in their southern neighbourhood that investment has been lagging behind.

When a situation is unfrozen and change does occur it can be for better or for worse, but then at least there will be a chance of improvement. This is when, building on the legitimacy that a policy of pragmatic idealism ought to have endowed them with, Europeans can actively attempt to generate multiplier effects, and to steer change in a direction that is beneficial to their interests. While Europe's preferred instruments are diplomatic and economic, military intervention is an option if change creates security concerns. A cost-benefit evaluation must determine, on a case-by-case basis, whether European military involvement is called for. If Europe does not intervene, will there be a threat against its vital interests? And what will be the humanitarian consequences for the population of the country itself? If it does intervene, what are the chances of averting the threat and creating the conditions in which change for the better can be consolidated? And what will be the risk of creating negative effects (such as escalation to other countries), of incurring casualties among European forces and collateral damage? In their own broad neighbourhood it will certainly increasingly be up to Europeans themselves to make that difficult calculation, to take the political initiative to develop a response, and to forge the coalition that can deliver it – for the US will no longer automatically do that for them.

Trade-offs are inevitable. When choosing to intervene militarily against Islamic State (IS) in Iraq and Syria, one cannot do without regional actors in the coalition, even if many of those countries themselves sustain practices (such as decapitating criminals and hanging homosexuals) that are absolutely at odds with universal values. Academics may try and develop elegant strategic concepts, but unfortunately elegance cannot always be preserved when conducting foreign and security policy. And yet these strategic concepts can help the EU to make decisions, to assess what is important for Europe and what is not, which responses are possible and which are not, and which resources ought to be allocated to them. Pragmatic idealism ought to ensure two things: that the EU remains true to universal egalitarian values and thus to itself, and that it plays an active, leading role. Sometimes taking the lead will lead to failure, but oftentimes it will lead to success – passively accepting the course of events will never.

Defence: And What Will Europe Do?

The need to think about when military action may be required automatically leads us to the next priority issue: how does Europe see its role in defence? Does anyone actually remember the original reason why the Common Security and Defence Policy of the EU was created?

It was certainly not so that the EU could have just one or two battalion-size battlegroups on stand-by (each provided by a Member State of group of Member States). Ever since the battlegroup scheme was launched, it has been a dominant theme in the deliberations on the CSDP. And it risks remaining so for a long time, for it presents a problem that cannot be solved. No matter how much the EU tries to perfect the scheme, the actual deployment of a battlegroup will always be a matter of coincidence: when a crisis occurs, does it fit the interests and political will, and the financial means, of the Member States whose forces happen to be on stand-by at that particular moment? Unless common funding is established and command authority over the battlegroups on stand-by is transferred to the Council, which could then decide on deployment by a majority vote, this is an insoluble conundrum. And thus the debate can go on and on – the perfect excuse not to have to talk about the actual objective of the CSDP.

At the inception of the CSDP, in 1999 (when it was still called the ESDP or European Security and Defence Policy, until the Lisbon Treaty introduced the name-change) Member States were much more ambitious. "To develop an autonomous capacity to take decisions and, where NATO as a whole is not engaged, to launch and conduct EU-led military operations in response to international crises": this was the purpose agreed upon by the European Council in Helsinki in 1999. The definition of the so-called "Petersberg Tasks" (after the conference site near Bonn in

Germany where they were first formulated) in the Treaty on European Union made clear that these operations include peace enforcement, i.e. war, alongside classic peacekeeping to prevent conflict from breaking out or resuming, military training and assistance to third countries, evacuation of EU citizens from danger zones, and support to humanitarian agencies in emergencies. To this end, the European Council defined the Headline Goal: the ambition to deploy up to a corps-size formation (50,000–60,000 troops), within one or two months, and to sustain it abroad for at least one year. However, the Headline Goal was last heard of during the 2008 French EU Presidency and has been completely overshadowed by the battlegroups. But even if the battlegroup scheme worked as desired, would that really greatly increase the EU's capacity to act? In which of the crises going on at the time of writing (Ukraine, Syria, Iraq, Libya, Mali…) would deploying a battalion-size battlegroup make a difference?

Clearly, the original *raison d'être* of the CSDP needs to be brought back to the attention of today's political, diplomatic and military decision-makers.

Unfortunately, ambiguity about the *raison d'être* was precisely the mechanism that made the CSDP possible in the first place. The CSDP is a Franco-British creation (something which the latter need to be reminded of more than the former). In 1998, at their annual bilateral meeting, held that year in St. Malo, the UK and France agreed to try and stimulate military capability development by launching a European scheme (Biscop, 2012). For Britain, the primary framework in which strategy would be set and decisions made on when and where to use those capabilities remained NATO. France believed that European capability development should also lead to autonomous European operations, outside the framework of NATO. Rather than eventually resolving itself, that fundamental ambiguity has continued to handicap the CSDP, which has never enjoyed the full support of all Member States. The end result is that it has never reached its full potential in either dimension: capability development or operations.

An elaborate process was conceived to fulfil the Headline Goal, and the European Defence Agency (EDA) was set up to urge Member States to invest in collective solutions for the priority shortfalls in the collective European arsenal. But by depriving the EDA of the budget to initiate projects itself, capitals have ensured that capability development remains an almost entirely bottom-up process, nearly completely reliant on national initiative and hence protective of national industrial interests. As a result, progress in addressing the shortfalls has been very slow indeed. Even so, as we shall see in chapter 3, the CSDP remains the most promising avenue for collective European capability development. Today though that promise is evident more because nations' performance in other frameworks is even more meagre than because of the CSDP's own achievements.

Elaborate institutions were also established to allow the EU to launch military operations and civilian missions – but not an operational headquarters, hence command and control of the military operations has to be outsourced to either NATO or a Member State. Nor has the EU been endowed with even sufficient planning capacity to do permanent prudent planning, i.e. a system in which planners, whenever something is brewing in an area of interest to Europe, start developing plans for different possible responses, diplomatic, economic as well as military, even before the political debate on what to do starts, so that if later politicians do decide to act, a final plan can be quickly developed. As a result, the EU's excellent intelligence and situational awareness (not least thanks to it encompassing network of embassies) is not consistently being translated in rapid response. The decision-making structure works for operations planned long in advance and sometimes even, if Member States want it to, for rapid reaction (in 2008 the EU deployed a civilian observer mission in Georgia in just a couple of weeks). But in general the lack of planning capacity and the slowness of decision-making mean that the EU is not systematically proactive enough to make it the platform of choice for addressing urgent security crises. Indeed, when fighting is expected, Member States, even those who regularly stress that the CSDP covers the full spectrum of military operations, rarely choose to deploy under the EU flag, but systematically opt for NATO or coalitions of the willing. The EU can perfectly plan for a military training mission to be deployed in Mali in six months, but if a crisis occurs today and troops need to deploy tomorrow, it cannot – which is exactly what happened in 2013.

In the end, it all boils down again to the issue of the *raison d'être*: What do the states of Europe really want to be able to do in security and defence? And how much of that do they want to do through the CSDP?

While Europeans themselves may remain undecided, the United States does not: as we have seen, it is pivoting to Asia. That pivot hinges on Europe: the more Europeans can take care of their own business, the more confidently the US can focus on Asia. Therefore the US does not only want Europeans to contribute to conventional deterrence under NATO's Article 5 and to American-led crisis management operations. In non-Article 5 scenarios around Europe, Washington expects Europeans themselves to initiate and lead crisis management in their periphery, preferably at an early stage, when a crisis has not yet escalated and can still be contained without relying too heavily on American assets. In other words, those Member States that are still seeking to please the US by curbing the development of the CSDP would be well advised to note that Washington now wants European defence to happen. Under which flag Europeans do something, the US does not care, as long as they do it. So whether it is NATO, the CSDP or an ad hoc coalition that takes charge, it will increasingly have to be Europeans who take the initiative.

The strategic situation thus ought to compel Europeans to revive their original ambition for autonomy and to reassess the role of the various foundations of the European security architecture: the EU and its CSDP, NATO, and the nations. Ultimately there is only one security architecture and the issue is not which part of it does what, but whether what has to be done gets done, with maximum effectiveness and efficiency. A new strategy should urgently define the level of ambition. Which responsibilities does Europe want to assume as a security provider outside its borders? How many capabilities is it willing to contribute to that end?

An Energetic Climate Change Policy

Short of nuclear war, the potentially most destructive challenges, not just to Europe but to human progress as such, are energy scarcity and global warming. Ian Morris (2010) argues (most convincingly as well as wittily) how since the origins of mankind, its development has been conditioned by nature and geography, and by its own technological progress, which allows it to adapt to nature and geography – or not. Development basically means that more people stay alive and live longer. When development hits a technological ceiling, it does not just stagnate but recedes, and population numbers fall down. Energy scarcity is precisely such a technological ceiling which it becomes urgent to break through, especially as in the wake of the Fukushima disaster, relying on nuclear energy appears ever less desirable. Though it would seem advisable not to abandon nuclear energy too soon, before alternatives are available: looking for them will be ever so much easier if the light stays on.

While global actors are competing for access to the remaining fossil fuels, finding the technological solution to break through the ceiling need not be a zero-sum game. Indeed, if the breakthrough is not realized, all great powers will be affected equally disastrously. If that happens, it will not then matter much whether until that point Europe or the US or China controlled the last fuel reserves, for development will be finished for all. With regard to climate change, it is even clearer that we live in an interpolar age: no great power could mitigate the consequences of global warming on its own, even if it wanted to, though the powers have yet to prove that they do want to do so collectively.

A great part of the challenge is domestic, notably requiring investment in research and technology. In addition Europe needs to create a real single market in energy, an "energy union" as the Commission is now envisaging. If all national grids are linked up and shortages in one EU Member State can be quickly compensated by transporting surpluses from another, Europe becomes a lot less amenable to blackmail from outside energy suppliers. For though some Member States are nearly fully dependent on a single supplier, no single supplier is powerful enough to menace the Union as a whole – if the grids are joined up. In addition to these internal measures, EU foreign policy needs to mitigate the short term effects of energy scarcity and climate change, for example by further diversifying the sources of supply (whereas the US is seeking energy self-sufficiency), and stepping up conflict prevention efforts to offset the multiplier effect of climate change on tension and conflict within and between states.

With Russia specifically, energy supply is a crucial dimension of the relationship. Putin will hopefully have provided enough of a scare to have convinced the EU Member States to finally fully integrate their energy markets and accelerate diversification of supply. But even when it achieves substantial diversification, the EU would do well to still buy Russian gas. It would then be in a much stronger position, able to demonstrate its goodwill by continued purchasing from and investment in the Russian energy sector, which is important for the stability of the country, but in the knowledge that it could much more easily turn its energy supply around. Europe's vulnerability *vis-à-vis* Russian energy blackmail would thus be much decreased.

Bilateral Partnerships for Effective Multilateralism

In 2003 the US invaded and occupied Iraq. In 2014 Russia invaded Ukraine and annexed the Crimea. Seen from Brasilia or New Delhi, the difference between both cases is not very obvious. That is why even the democratic emerging powers like Brazil and India prefer not to pronounce either way on either case, in spite of their professed adherence to the principle of non-intervention. China certainly avoids taking a clear public stance on the Ukraine crisis, even though it was an Asian airliner (Malaysian Airlines flight MH17) that was shot down over Ukraine in the summer of 2014 and it might very well have been a Chinese aircraft. But Beijing finds itself in too comfortable a position: with the EU, the US and Russia engaged in a serious dispute, China can sit back and reap the benefits, such as the advantageous (to Beijing) gas deal that Russia hurriedly signed to demonstrate that it does not entirely rely on the European market. Outside Europe and the US, even the intervention in Libya in 2011 is often perceived as a transgression, in spite of the fact that Europeans and Americans intervened following a request from the Arab League, and with a UN mandate. All of this goes to show that Europe's legitimacy in the rest of the world is not necessarily as great as Europe often thinks it is, even in other democracies.

If Europe wants "effective multilateralism", the other major objective the ESS put forward in 2003, to work, it will have to invest a lot of effort in revamping its relations, especially with its strategic partners. One thing is sure: multilateralism, i.e. cooperation between the powers, is more difficult in an age of increased competition for dwindling resources between a growing number of global actors – which is exactly why it is even more important than in 2003. War between the powers would be disastrous for Europe's vital interests.

Europe has to return to a much more proactive multilateral stance therefore. Europeans are conscious of the imperfections of the current multilateral system: while they themselves are often over-represented, the emerging powers are under-represented in many bodies. In the international financial institutions for example, the Benelux countries still control more votes than China. Though I do not want to deny the genius of the Belgian, Dutch and Luxembourg peoples, reform is long overdue. Examples like this hamper the legitimacy and effectiveness of the system. At the same time, certain policy areas are insufficiently addressed by the current system, and lack institutions with the necessary competences and the power to enforce them. Europe ought to actively try and shape the reform of the system, rather than let the initiative to others. For the others have been active. In setting up their own organizations, but these have been not very successful. The examples of Russia's project for a Eurasian Union with the former Soviet republics and the Shanghai Cooperation Organization (SCO) convening Russia, China and Central Asia demonstrate that the desire to have a "no westerners allowed" club is insufficient to create a purposive and performing multilateral organization. Indeed, in 2015 China opted for an alternative road and invited western countries to join the Asian Infrastructure Investment Bank that it set up (Renard, 2015). Europeans wisely ignored American prodding not to and accepted the invitation, thus buying a say in the decision-making and ensuring that the new bank contributes rather than detracts from effective multilateralism. At the same time, many deplore Europe's *suivisme vis-à-vis* the US' TTIP initiative, which together with its Pacific counterpart, TTP, seeks to organize the world on a US-centred basis. Are we sure that this will aid rather than hamper effective multilateralism?

Effective multilateralism will remain a challenge. Many of the emerging powers adhere to the multilateralism of 1945: multilateral bodies as forums where the powers meet to settle their problems, rather than as institutions with powers in their own right. Europeans, formed by their own experience of EU integration, of course have a much more ambitious view of strong multilateral institutions that can impose binding rules. Furthermore the emerging powers do not agree among themselves. Though the emerging powers are quite obviously underrepresented in the Security Council, China is quite happy with its composition because it of course does have a permanent seat. The BRICS countries meet regularly among themselves, but have demonstrated their differences more often than their accord. This can be to Europe's benefit, for it would be very disadvantageous were the BRICS to be consolidated as a firm and cohesive grouping in opposition to the EU, the US and other "western powers". Instead, Europe should use its bilateral partnerships with all of them to forge ad hoc coalitions in different issue areas and work with different sets of countries wherever interests coincide. If it works with Russia and China on the nuclear negotiations with Iran, for example, perhaps on another issue it will find it can work with China and India.

An update of EU strategy could put this modus operandi forward, as well as indicate the priority issue areas in which Europe seeks to reinforce the multilateral system.

Conclusion

For too long a time, the states of Europe have avoided a real debate about their collective strategy. Yet they could not avoid doing strategy in the real world. Confronted with the crises in their near abroad, to name just the most obviously pressing example, a course of action had to be chosen. For most European governments today, the option is to act together or not to act at all. But even a choice for inaction still is strategic behaviour: a policy choice with long-term effects on the values and interests of the policy-maker. Those states that retain a significant national strategic posture are quickly running out of means and thus out of options unless they can spur more countries to act alongside them. They may choose to do that on ad hoc basis, crisis by crisis and region by region, but if they want to be sure of achieving the required critical mass, they must seek a European strategic consensus.

Strategic behaviour can be improvised, but its effects are more likely to be positive if the policy-maker debates and decides on strategy beforehand. To quote Colin Gray once more:

> The only difference between having and not having an explicit grand strategy, lies in the degree of cohesion of official behaviours and, naturally as a consequence of poor cohesion, in the likelihood of success. (2010, p. 28)

Chapter 2
Power Struggles in Europe's Neighbourhood: Game of Zones

Europe's neighbourhood has rarely been quiet. The post-Cold War era was inaugurated by a civil war on Europe's eastern borders, in Yugoslavia, and by an inter-state war in its southern periphery, when Iraq invaded Kuwait. In the 25 years since there has rarely been a year without conflict in one or other of Europe's neighbours. It is striking therefore how surprised Europeans appeared at the turn of events in their broad neighbourhood in these last few years. True, in 2015 many crises coincide (at the time of writing in Iraq, Libya, Syria, Ukraine, Yemen…), which reduces the available bandwidth to address every single one of them, and thus enhances the pervasive sense that we are continuously running after the facts. Today IS posts another massacre an YouTube and all eyes turn south; the next day rebels storm another city in eastern Ukraine and all attention shifts back east, and so on and so forth.

But to speak of game-changers that have altered the face of European security is to overstate the case. Algeria in the 1990s already demonstrated how religious extremism can fuel a gruesome civil war and how easily that can spill over to Europe, with terrorist attacks hitting France. The wars in Afghanistan, and later Chechnya and Iraq, already showed how religiously framed conflict can attract foreign combatants. The Russo-Georgian war ought to have made us understand that at least since 2008, if not before, Moscow regarded itself to be engaged in a zero-sum game and was willing to use force to preserve what it regards as its sphere of interest. And is not hybrid warfare a modus operandi that during the Cold War both sides excelled at, combining propaganda, infiltration and other covert operations to combat hostile regimes?

Had Europe, the US and Russia established a true partnership of trust, that would truly have been a game-changer, but that window of opportunity has been closed for now. The brief interval in which that seemed to be in the cards already ended in the early 2000s. Not for the first time in history Europe now sees Russia as a great power that it dare not trust. But it is no longer such a great power that it actually threatens Europe's own territory. Consequently, the stand-off about Ukraine also does not threaten global stability in a truly multipolar world, in which notably China is much more powerful than Russia, to the extent that a similar crisis would have during the Cold War.

This is not to say that there is no need for concern – it is just to put that concern into perspective. The only direct threat of violence against EU and NATO territory is terrorism, fuelled by the wars to the south of Europe. But nobody is plotting a military invasion of Europe, including Russia, if only because nobody has the military capability. Europe is right to bemoan the state of its armed forces (as we will see in the next chapter), but those of Russia are even worse off. The crack units involved in the take-over of the Crimea are not representative for the full 770,000 – compared to the 1,500,000 people that the 28 EU members still have in uniform. And of course Europe, through NATO, is ensured against invasion because of American nuclear and conventional deterrence in addition to Europe's own forces. So invading an EU or NATO member would be a different ball game, more importantly because seen from Moscow their actions in Ukraine are their ball game. In its view, Russia is not interfering in a foreign country, but setting its house in order. That is why it refuses to accept interference from Europe and the US, but that is also why the incursion into Ukraine should not be misunderstood as a threat to the EU and NATO themselves.

Compared to any moment in European history since the fall of the West Roman Empire, Europe is in a luxurious situation. One should never rest on one's laurels, to pursue the Roman image. Europe's trade, its energy supply and the security of its citizens living abroad are all at stake in its neighbourhood, and mass refugee flows and the spilling over of violence affect its own territory as well. The crises in Europe's neighbourhood have to be managed therefore, before they threaten Europe itself – which is not yet the case. One can understand that the EU feels ill at ease in this "game of zones", because as seen in the previous chapter, it is rediscovering strategic thinking. With an assertive Russia trying to establish an exclusive zone of influence in the east and IS taking control of a large zone in the south this clearly is a game for high stakes. The European Neighbourhood Policy has obviously been unsuccessful in stabilizing Europe's periphery. But is Europe really as ill-equipped to play the game as it feels?

No More Quiet on the Eastern and Southern Fronts

To look east first: many Europeans had forgotten or had pushed to the back of their minds all the indications of Russian dissatisfaction with the perceived western encroachment on its near abroad. The view was widespread that Georgian President Mikheil Saakashvili had brought the 2008 war with Russia upon himself (which is perhaps not entirely without truth), and afterwards relations with Russia went back to normal very quickly. Russian pleas for a revised, more inclusive European security architecture were *encommissioné* in the OSCE, buried in a lengthy discussion process that Europeans and Americans never expected to lead to any conclusion, in an organization that many diplomats derided as the Organization for Seminars and Conferences in Europe (rather than Security and Cooperation). Europeans preferred to believe that they were not engaged in a zero-sum game in their eastern neighbourhood.

Seen from Brussels, that view was of course correct. The EU did not decide at some point that it wanted Ukraine, or any other eastern neighbour, for itself. The EU's hope was that these countries of *Zwischeneuropa*, wedged in between itself and Russia, would be able to make their own choices, instead of Brussels or Moscow choosing for them. If they would choose to develop close ties with Europe, the EU would gladly oblige, on the condition that they would undertake economic reforms and commit to improve democracy, respect for human rights and the rule of law. But the EU never asked that they would sever relations with Russia. Russia however does not see the world through this lens. Moscow wants an exclusive sphere of interest. Because a win-win situation requires that both sides perceive a benefit, Europe and Russia *were* engaged in a zero-sum game, whether the Europeans wanted to or not.

Those who deride Europe for failing to understand that it was stumbling into a zero-sum game, especially in the US, are not entirely wrong. The ENP was simply not political enough. A focus on the "low politics" of economic and technical cooperation, to the detriment of the "high politics" of diplomacy and defence; a wide range of ongoing activities, but without a strategy linking these to well-defined political ends: these were the consequences of the EU's conscious avoidance of any fundamental debate on how to deal with Russia, for fear of bringing out the divisions between its Member States. Activities under the flag of the Eastern Partnership, the multilateral dimension of the EU's engagement with its eastern periphery, went on without it being clear which relationship the EU eventually aspired to with the six countries concerned. Unfortunately, one must repeat that activity is no substitute for strategy: if you do not know what your objectives are, even the most diverse array of activities is unlikely to achieve them – and may produce undesirable side effects.

Throughout 2013, warnings were issued by EU Member States' embassies in Kiev and from within the EU apparatus itself (notably the EEAS) that appearances were deceptive and that the signing of the envisaged agreement with Ukraine would not proceed that smoothly, for domestic political reasons first of all. Implementing its far-reaching and extremely complex stipulations was in fact incompatible with the nature of the regime – any Ukrainian regime, given the country's weak governance structures. Pushing on regardless, the EU set in motion a chain of events that led to an (itself unpredictable) Russian overreaction when the domestic political crisis in Ukraine escalated into massive demonstrations against President Viktor Yanukovych. Thus Europe learned about the geopolitical implications of technical cooperation, export of norms and trade relations the hard way.

Yet one should not judge too harshly either. That people demonstrated *en masse* on the Maidan Square in Kiev for closer association with the EU, even if they did instrumentalize that in their protest against Yanukovich, means that what the EU stands for and what if offers through the ENP is attractive. One wishes that people in London would go out into the streets and demand more Europe. One can say therefore that in a way the ENP worked in Ukraine: even if in the case of Ukraine the tactics were faulty, the basic strategic premise was correct.

Besides, it has already been forgotten that just a few years ago, in 2006–2008, the Europeans prevented the US from making exactly the same mistake, when they resisted President George W. Bush's push for NATO membership for Ukraine and Georgia. Surely that move would not have remained without a Russian reaction either. Alas, neither Washington nor Brussels seems to have learned very much from that episode. In fact, at the time Ukraine itself eventually declined to join NATO. That ought to have taught both Europe and the US that when a country itself is too divided over its own future, pushing it to make an untimely choice is unwise, for it is bound to increase domestic tensions.

And those tensions are easily exploited by Ukraine's other neighbour, Russia, seeking to advance its pawns in the "game of zones". Russia is acting more out of weakness than out of strength, however. Rather than executing a master plan, Russian President Vladimir Putin seems to be making it up as he goes along. He has proved very apt at putting Europeans and Americans off balance, by taking actions that while greatly perturbing always stayed below a certain threshold (such as incursions by the so-called "little green men"), so that Brussels and Washington remain in doubt over the correct reaction. That makes Putin a brilliant tactician, but he is not the master strategist. He supported Yanukovych to the very end, probably because he did not see an alternative way of safeguarding Russian influence. Then Yanukovych fled the country (21 February 2014), in spite of an agreement with the opposition brokered by the foreign ministers of France, Germany and Poland. Either he did so without prior warning to Moscow, which means Russia lost control of events, or with Russian connivance, in which case Putin gravely miscalculated. For immediately the Ukrainian opposition filled the void and came to power, and naturally turned to its western neighbour for support. At a stroke, Putin lost most of his influence in Ukraine.

The subsequent Russian annexation of the Crimea can be seen as an overreaction. The peninsula's only strategic asset is the naval base, the continued Russian use of which the new Ukrainian government guaranteed right away. But it is typical of a bully to grab by force even what he could get by asking politely, because that is what the bully's reputation depends on. The Russian defence attaché who, having listened to me at a conference, came to find me in order to insist that Russia is a great power because it has nuclear weapons and can destroy any country in the world is illustrative of this mind-set. Nuclear power, of course; soft power…? The legitimacy of the regime is based to a great extent on the pretence that Russia remains a great power on a par with the US and China. Much more than that Putin cannot offer to his population, for the economy is too weak. The easiest way of maintaining that mirage is by acting as a spoiler in the West, simply because we in the West are such polite company. It is difficult to imagine Putin taking similar risks *vis-à-vis* China, which would likely react with somewhat less circumspection than Europe and the US. When Ukraine suddenly tilted towards the West, Putin probably had to act, to preserve the standing of the regime. But to take on a bigger part than that of spoiler, be it a very irritating one, Russia no longer has the means – and even then it should probably be careful not to bite off more than it can chew.

The real game-changer for Europe and the security of its neighbourhood is that the US has made the same assessment of Russian strength and has reoriented its strategy accordingly, hence the pivot to Asia, where in China the Americans see their only potential strategic competitor. The not so implicit message to Europe is perfectly logical: Europeans must assume a lot more responsibility for security in their own neighbourhood. The "European Reassurance Initiative" that President Obama announced in early June 2014, asking Congress for $1 billion to temporarily deploy additional American forces to Eastern Europe, organize exercises and train allies and partners, was meant to underscore this message. Rather than a reversal of the pivot, it said to Europeans, in the run-up to the NATO summit in Wales in September of the same year: shame on you, for you ought to be doing this yourself.

The situation in Europe's southern neighbourhood presents much more of a potential game-changer. At first in the positive sense, when for an all too brief moment it seemed that the Arab Spring, which started in Tunisia in late 2010, would herald an era of democratization. But then in the negative sense, as it turned out to be more of a Belgian spring: stormy and unpredictable. Civil wars and the risk of fragmentation in several states are intertwined with proxy wars between Saudi Arabia and Iran, which are competing for dominance of the Gulf region, but at the same time are unlikely allies against the common enemy of IS, which in turn seeks to do away with the existing states altogether. A permanent IS "caliphate" and/or a dismantling of several states into Bantustans supported by either Saudi Arabia or Iran (Ali, 2015, p. 21) would be a recipe for long-term instability.

At first sight, the EU's Neighbourhood Policy seems to have suffered from the same weakness in the south as in the east, which led to the EU being overtaken by the Arab Spring just as much as by the crisis in Ukraine. But while in the east a technocratic focus on "low politics" masked the actual absence of an EU strategy, a closer look reveals that in the south "low politics" masked a very much "high politics" approach by the EU – but one that was also very much at odds with the rhetoric of the ENP. Not so much the absence of strategy as the discrepancy between the declared and the actual strategy handicapped the EU. In practice, the ambitious ENP agenda of stimulating neighbouring governments to equally provide for all their citizens in terms of security, prosperity and freedom in return for more access to European markets was abandoned in favour of a short-term focus on energy, illegal migration, and terrorism. Whichever regime was ready to cooperate with the EU in these areas could count on its support, quite regardless of the human rights situation. The former colonial powers' special relationships with most countries of the region did not help the EU to maintain more of a critical distance. As a result pictures featuring embarrassing embraces with since ousted dictators can be found of quite a few European leaders. Thus in the end the EU no longer adhered to its own principles. This was the context in which obviously flawed elections in for example pre-Arab Spring Tunisia did not lead to condemnations but to congratulations. Compare with the EU imposition of sanctions on Belarus after equally flawed elections. The EU was very slow to relinquish this attitude and to welcome the revolutions in Tunisia and Egypt (as was the US). Restoring the European image in the region after this initial hesitant stance was one of the motivations of the military intervention when the Arab Spring reached Libya.

Tony Judt (2008: 365) was addressing Kissinger and US foreign policy when he wrote down these lines, originally in 1998, but in an uncanny way they fit the European Union of 2011 faced with the Eurozone crisis and the Arab Spring:

> … in a constitutionally ordered state, where laws are derived from broad principles of right and wrong and where those principles are enshrined in and protected by agreed procedures and practices, it can never be in the long-term interest of the state or its citizens to flout those procedures at home or associate too closely overseas with the enemies of your founding ideals.

Had the EU remained true to its principles, the region probably would not have seen a speedier or less violent transition. Belarus has not seen any democratization either. But the EU would have enjoyed much greater legitimacy and could have been a source of inspiration and support for those opposing authoritarianism, as it still can be *vis-à-vis* dissidents in Minsk. In Tunisia people rose in revolt demanding exactly what Europe stands for, but contrary to people in Ukraine, they saw the EU as an obstacle rather than an ally in their struggle. Thus if to a certain extent the ENP can be said to have worked in Europe's eastern neighbourhood, in the south it largely failed. One positive conclusion can nevertheless be drawn. Revolution and protest in both the Eastern and Southern neighbourhood of Europe have vindicated the core *idea* of EU foreign policy. An equal share in security, prosperity and freedom is a universal demand and not a European or western conception; without it, no durable peace and stability are possible.

No Neighbourhood Policy Without a Security Policy

Europe needs a new Neighbourhood Policy (Lehne, 2008), one that is adapted to the new realities in its periphery. Adapting does not mean that Europe too should start playing the classic "game of zones" and try and establish an exclusive sphere of influence, as other actors are trying to do. The best way of preserving EU interests is not to attempt to bring Europe's neighbours under its control. As Russia is learning in Ukraine, even if part of the population supports you, you will inevitably antagonize others, which is a recipe for perennial instability. EU interests are better served by empowering its neighbours to make their own choices, and to offer mutually beneficial partnership if they also, but not exclusively, choose to cooperate with Europe. The EU does not need its neighbours to look up to it, but it does not want them to look away from it either – that would be very harmful for its interests. Empowerment starts with domestic stability, which starts with integrating all citizens in the political arena, guaranteeing their security, and their share in the wealth of the country. The EU certainly does not need to abandon the core idea of the European Security Strategy therefore.

Before any new long-term regional policies can be put in place however, the EU must address the ongoing crises in its neighbourhood.

To start with Europe must make it absolutely clear that it does consider the security of this broad region to be its responsibility. Not just because that is what the US expects, but in the first place because the EU's comprehensive regional policies will not be credible if the impression persists, as in the past, that its engagement ends where hard security problems begin. Trade and aid and democracy promotion rarely thrive in countries at war. Europe must be the first-line security provider in its own neighbourhood. That means that whenever a security problem arises, the EU must take the lead, assess the situation, decide how important it is in view of its interests, initiate a response, and forge a coalition to deliver it. In many instances a diplomatic response will be called for, at which the High Representative and the EEAS have already proven to be proficient. For example Catherine Ashton brokered a deal between Serbs and Kosovars; the EU's leading role in the Iran negotiations is another example. Diplomacy can be supplemented as required with sticks and carrots from the comprehensive EU toolkit (trade, development, SSR, sanctions, etc.).

But Europeans, through the EU, NATO or ad hoc coalitions, must also display the ability and the will to use force, first of all as a credible deterrent that will enhance the effectiveness of its diplomacy. Actual military intervention is the last resort when vital interests and/or the responsibility to protect cannot otherwise be upheld. Even if the EU would formally declare the broader neighbourhood a security priority, at the level of grand strategy, whether or not to intervene in a specific crisis will always depend on an ad hoc cost-benefit calculation. What positive effects could intervention achieve, but which negative fall-out might it generate and which risks would our forces run? Crucial to the military success of recent interventions (in Libya and Mali) is notably that a major part of the population welcomed them. If that support is lost, or is not there in the first place, no military intervention can produce long-term effects. Even if it has popular support, the long-term success of intervention is not guaranteed, because paradoxically the resulting government can be delegitimized by the very fact that it could not have come into being without external support (Doyle, 2015, p. 26). And of course, no military intervention should be undertaken unless it is part of a comprehensive political, economic and security approach. It will in any case be a *European* decision. As a consequence of the pivot, the US will no longer take the initiative in Europe's place but will look to Europeans to take charge.

These long-term security obligations provide the framework for the EU's short-term crisis management.

The EU undoubtedly contributed to deepening the domestic political crisis in Ukraine, but once it became an international crisis, because of the Russian intervention, Europe actually has responded pretty adequately. The EU adopted sanctions to signal its dissatisfaction with the annexation of the Crimea, and initially kept further sanctions in reserve to warn Putin against similar military incursion in mainland Ukraine. It provided economic support to the Ukrainian government and helped to organize the presidential elections, and European leaders engaged in high-level diplomacy with Putin, notably during their meeting at the commemoration of the Allied landing in Normandy in June 2014. Indeed, Obama aligned himself with this approach in his Brussels speech on 26 March 2014, putting paid to rather more belligerent utterings in some American quarters. Just to illustrate some of these other voices, I heard a senior colleague of a prominent American think tank call for the deployment of nuclear weapons in the Baltic states – as if that was going to de-escalate tension – and that was a think-tank leaning to the Democrats. Of course, EU decisions were preceded by difficult debates between Member States, but that should not overshadow the outcome. In spite of the fact that Russia is actively trying to play off one Member State against another, and that in several Member States it carries great economic weight, the 28 have at the time of writing maintained unity.

In spite of the initial set of sanctions, Russian forces did infiltrate Eastern Ukraine. There was a movement in favour of greater decentralization, but without Russian intervention this most likely would not have turned into an armed rebellion against the government in Kiev. The separatist rebels forced the EU's hand when in a fatal mistake they shot down Malaysian airliner MH17 on 17 July 2014, with missiles that could only have been provided by Russia. Confronted with the death of 298 innocent civilians, many of them EU citizens, the EU could not possibly not react, and imposed additional (mostly financial) sanctions that hurt. Unfortunately, Putin did not use this opportunity to quietly phase out his support for the armed separatists without too much loss of face – a factor that is crucial to the acceptability of any outcome to Moscow. The MH17 disaster damaged Russia's international position. Though Russia's usual partners still did not pronounce any public condemnation, they could hardly be seen to condone the death of so many innocent civilians.

The crisis persisted, and still does when I am writing this, even though German Chancellor Angela Merkel, with French President François Hollande, brokered yet another ceasefire agreement, Minsk II (11 February 2015), with Putin, which should lead to a final settlement (elections in the east are to be followed by Kiev resuming control of the external border, across which Russian military support has been passing freely). Minsk II was very important in keeping the US on the diplomatic track: impatience in many quarters in the US seems to belie the pivot. If Merkel and Hollande had not showed leadership, Obama may have felt under pressure to fill the perceived void – and would not necessarily have acted in accordance with European interests. Yet, as before, the rebellion was allowed (by Russia) to continue, in spite of Minsk II, but not to escalate beyond a certain threshold. Furthermore, only rather weak counter-sanctions were adopted by Russia to the sanctions imposed by Europe and the US. The threat to stop importing second-hand cars from Europe is hardly indicative of great power status – and even that threat was not made hard. The energy weapon cannot really be used by either side, for it is a double-edged sword: Russia is as dependent on European revenue and investment as Europe is on Russian gas. Putin too seems to have noticed that in eastern Ukraine there may be a lot of dissatisfaction with rule from Kiev, but it is neither as massive as (it apparently is) in the Crimea nor does it necessarily equate with a wish to join Russia. Unlike in the Crimea therefore, pushing things to extremes may lead to a bloody and protracted civil war (as civil wars usually are) in which Putin likely prefers not to be involved. Instead the military stand-off is being maintained, with low-level violence going on continually and with occasional new thrusts, which then fizzle out again – just enough to keep Ukraine, and Europe and the US, continually off-balance. Russia may in fact have more interest in keeping Ukraine together but weak, which creates opportunities to wield influence nationally, rather than in splitting off further parts, which would cut it off completely from the Western-oriented country that would remain (Wood, 2014). Therefore, Russia seems to be aiming at adding another "frozen conflict" to the list.

That also implies that the EU and the US can aid Ukraine to build up its armed forces, notably by offering training and equipment, but with the objective of resisting offensive moves by the separatists and of preparing for the ultimate restoration of order throughout the country and of the central government's control over all external borders, as provided for by the Minsk II agreement. The objective should not be to try and resolve the issue by force. Thou shalt not arm those who cannot win. If arming Ukraine would lead to it taking up the offensive, every additional military effort would just be matched by Russia step-by-step, and the result would still be the same stalemate – only more people would be killed. Europeans (and Americans) are not willing to go to war over Ukraine themselves. Then they should not go down a road that would lead to more war, for fighting to the last Ukrainian is not a very honourable position. Furthermore, if the West would seek escalation, Russia might then be tempted to escalate the conflict beyond Ukraine after all, not as an end in its own right but as a means of pressure, by stirring up trouble in the Baltic states for example. In the same vein, Europe should not over-react to Russian military posturing (such as overflights): it is but posturing, in order not to create the impression that Russia is scared off by the strong declarations emanating from NATO since the Wales Summit, and it probably indicates a rising nervousness inside the regime because of the dire effect of sanctions on the economy.

All that the EU can do is to maintain sanctions and at the same time to continue its diplomatic engagement to try and forge a consensus on a federal solution for Ukraine that can satisfy all Ukrainians, including in the East of the country, which can therefore also be a face-saving way out for Russia. As a Belgian, I would just say: do not push decentralization too far ... A commitment by the Ukrainian government not to apply for NATO membership could be part of an honourable deal and, as George Kennan (quoted in Gaddis, 2011, p. 674) said of the states of eastern Europe: "the only safe way to establish their true independence is to show a decent respect for [Russian] security interests". In any case, most allies do not currently want Ukraine to join NATO, if they are honest about it. Only when the Ukrainian government has effective control of all outside borders of mainland Ukraine, can sanctions be lifted. Above all, EU Member States must maintain unity.

Nonetheless, there is a painful moral dilemma here. Although democratization is difficult to engineer from the outside, as we have seen, when it does happen it is always in Europe's interest to support it, especially in a case like Ukraine where people explicitly demand a close association with the EU and where the EU has actively encouraged this. When that democratic and European aspiration then leads to aggression by another power, Europe definitely has a moral duty to lend help. Yet if helping Ukraine leads only to an escalation of the war, that is in the interest of neither Europe nor Ukraine itself. Nevertheless, one understands only too well that many in Ukraine feel deserted by the West. In the end though, the outcome of the crisis might still be relatively positive: the gradual stabilization of a more democratic Ukraine, free to build constructive relations with all of its neighbours. The downside for Europe will be that, with the US and the international financial institutions, it will likely have to foot the bill for a long time to come. The economic and political challenges in Ukraine are huge. Success is by no means guaranteed: the country already had one chance to establish good governance after the 2004 "coloured revolution" – and lost it.

If the Minsk II agreement works out completely, "mainland" Ukraine will be reunited in its entirety under the control of the Kiev government. Unfortunately it remains very possible that the rebel-held enclaves in the east will end up as another "frozen conflict". What the EU will definitely not achieve is to return the Crimea to Ukraine – note that it goes unmentioned in the Minsk II agreement. The peninsula will join South Ossetia and Abkhazia in Georgia, and others, in the category of territories whose proclaimed status Europe does not formally recognize but also does not actively attempt to alter. That is unsatisfactory, but it ought not to be a surprise. The history of international relations since World War Two shows that the Permanent Five do not wage war against one another, and that even proxy wars between other actors that they support tend to be very costly for all sides. Just as, earlier in this century, Russia and China protested against but could do little in practice to end the evidently illegal US invasion and occupation of Iraq, so the balance of power impels us to live with a Russian Crimea, however much we disapprove.

The question that Europe should ask itself is: is it willing to establish as close relations and spend as much treasure on the other countries of the Eastern Partnership? If they so desire, of course. In the case of Moldova a positive answer seems already guaranteed from both sides. As regards Belarus the question does not now pose itself, but we have seen that autocratic regimes can crumble quite unexpectedly. But what about the South Caucasus? What are their aspirations, how far is Europe willing to go to meet them, and how can it avoid another clash with Russia? At the same time, Russia may have damaged its own long-term interests, for even those who are inclined to look to Moscow rather than to Brussels did not count on cessation of territory being part of the bargain, as happened to Ukraine.

The security situation to the east of Europe cannot be called predictable, but at least the number of players is limited. The opposite is true about Europe's southern periphery, where the situation has become very complex indeed.

In recent years, awareness has sharply increased across the EU that security in the broader southern neighbourhood concerns all of the 28 Member States. That does not yet translate, unfortunately, into a great and universal willingness to act when forceful intervention is required. In Libya in 2011 and again in Mali in 2013 ad hoc coalitions outside the EU had to take the military lead, at the initiative of Britain and France, with the EU as such not coming onto the stage until the follow-up phase. But the EU does now have comprehensive regional strategies for the Sahel and the Horn, in the implementation of which is has deployed military as well as civilian training and capacity-building missions and of course the naval operation Atalanta. It also deployed a border assistance mission in Libya. Furthermore, it attempted to play a vital role in the diplomatic processes to end the civil war in Syria and effectively did so in the case of the nuclear negotiations with Iran. The success of none of these engagements was guaranteed in the first place, but turmoil in the region reached another level with the military take-over of significant parts of Syria and Iraq by IS in 2014. What is required first of all is staying power: the will and the means to sustain engagement (diplomatic, economic, military) until an acceptable end-state has been achieved.

The security situation in the Sahel appears manageable, but fighting in Mali remains endemic and the EU will have to sustain its military deployment as well as its economic and financial support for years to come if the region is not to slide back into major instability. Politically, EU engagement remains instrumental to stability and governance. Militarily, the vastness of the region is a challenge, but on the other hand even a limited number of major assets (notably air support) in support of local forces can make a difference as insurgents are mostly but lightly equipped. The EU has come to realize that in addition to sending instructors to train the local armed forces and police, equipping them with the necessary hardware will often be a precondition for success. In any case, training another country's military until they reach a level of effectiveness comparable to European troops is a very long-term project. In the Horn of Africa, the efforts of years in this sense are finally bearing fruit, but here too a sustained effort is necessary. It will be some time to come before Somalia is sufficiently stable and prosperous to eradicate the root causes of piracy. Until that time the EU has no choice but to keep patrolling the neighbouring waters or else the moment its ships leave the pirates will quickly reappear.

Much more challenging is the situation in Libya. The fact that after the military intervention in 2011 the country slid back into civil war is often used as an example of the futility of intervention, but the opposite is true. Militarily, the intervention was a complete success, but its effects have been completely negated by gravely deficient political and economic follow-up. The EU is not the only one to be blamed; there was also a very timid UN and the absence of a clear centre of power in the country, but the latter made it all the more urgent to act. Eventually, after arduous negotiations, the EU deployed a border assistance mission (May 2013), but by then the situation had become far too chaotic and dangerous for it to be more than a token deployment, and not even that once it was withdrawn to Tunisia (August 2014). The crisis in Mali has already demonstrated the damage that spill-over from Libya can cause; in turn Libya was then affected by spill-over from Syria and Iraq, as IS elements established themselves in the country.

Helping Libya to establish peace and stability is an obvious example of an issue for which the EU much more than any other outside actor must assume primary responsibility. Though success is by no means guaranteed, the EU has the most instruments to work with the Libyan authorities to try and create a semblance of stability. That implies a much more ambitious role than it is assuming at the time of writing, first of all in the diplomatic field, in order to bring the competing centres of power to the negotiating table and try and establish a unity government. In situations like this, Europe must be ready to consider the options for renewed militarily action, ideally peacekeeping to guarantee a ceasefire (in the Libyan case, after a unity government has come into being) but if necessary well-circumscribed peace enforcement if the political objective cannot be achieved by any other means. Restoring a degree of government control in Libya is also the only real means of stemming the tide of desperate migrants risking their lives crossing the Mediterranean, often at the mercy of ruthless human traffickers and in hazardous and overcrowded craft. Stepped-up naval operations will rescue more lives, and will destroy some of the traffickers' assets, but cannot address the heart of the matter.

The gravest crisis is the civil war in Syria and Iraq. Initially military intervention in Syria was calculated to cause more harm than good. Even the use of chemical weapons did not affect this calculus, as President Obama's final reluctance to use force demonstrated. The war however has proved too intractable for the diplomatic process to achieve anything beyond the destruction of chemical weapons – a good thing, but it does not in itself stop the war. At least spill-over of violence to where it was most feared (to Lebanon, Jordan and Turkey) has so far been limited, but the risk remains; military action in support of their armed forces may yet be called for to prevent spill-over to any of these three countries from materializing. Meanwhile the neighbouring countries are doing the best they can to cope with a massive refugee crisis with what hardly seems sufficient aid from the international community, including Europe.

In June 2014 the war spectacularly hit Iraq, when the extremist IS that was fighting Assad in Syria took everyone by surprise by capturing large parts of northern Iraq. Another proof (if more was needed) of the error of invading Iraq in 2003 and of the complete and utter failure to establish a well-functioning state ever since. But though the US did create it, Europe cannot consider this to be just an American problem, for the stability of the entire Middle East is at stake if IS cannot be contained. Furthermore, IS is exactly the group that many fighters originating from Europe have joined, hence Europeans have a responsibility to contribute, and a clear security interest, as several people have returned from the theatre of war to commit or plan acts of terrorism on European soil. Of course domestic measures are indispensable: continued vigilance by police and intelligence services to avert terrorist attacks; engagement with groups at risk of indoctrination to prevent more young Europeans from becoming "foreign fighters"; reintegration into society of those who return from the conflict zone; and, ultimately, a serious look at European society to understand how Europe's own citizens can become so alienated from it. But if European governments are pretending to their citizens that these domestic measures alone will bring security, they are deceiving them. Jihadist terrorism cannot be separated from the international geopolitical and ideological context that inspires it.

The primary responsibility for fighting IS lies with the states of the region, for the security of these regimes is directly at stake, even though many of them initially channelled support to IS. They are certainly not the only ones to have created their own greatest enemy (someone should write a book on Frankenstein and International Relations), but that does not absolve them from their responsibility. Meanwhile decision-makers in Europe, while wringing their hands about the war in Syria, tried very much not to look at Iraq – that was an American problem, not theirs – hence their surprise when IS made Syria and Iraq into a single theatre of war. The rapidity of IS advance forced the US, with European support, to cobble together a coalition of the not so able and rather unwilling from the region, united only because they fear IS even more than each other, and to launch air strikes to prevent Iraq from falling into IS hands altogether. Very much to their surprise, several European states now found themselves in Iraq (at the invitation of its government, and not in Syria, in the absence of a UN mandate), with combat aircraft and even military trainers on the ground. Several countries from the region participate as well, but overall the perception remains that of another Western intervention.

What has been achieved at the time of writing? The territorial expansion of IS seems to be contained, at least in Iraq, but the area under their control can only be retaken by ground forces. In Syria, the losing party is not so much IS as the other opposition groups, who are being fought by both IS and the Assad regime. The latter is in no position to regain any lost territories, but it certainly is not being defeated either. At most, the air campaign has produced an uneasy stalemate. That is not synonymous with failure: without the western intervention, IS would most likely have grabbed even more territory before, if ever, the hesitant regimes in the region would have been stirred into action. It is likely that external actors will remain crucial to forge broad coalitions and promote diplomatic solutions, if situations as in Yemen are to be avoided, where when renewed fighting broke out in the spring of 2015 Saudi Arabia and Iran began a proxy war by supporting opposite sides, with scant regard for the security of civilians. How strong a role the US will play in the future is difficult to predict; against America's long-term involvement and clear interests in the region stands intervention fatigue, particularly *vis-à-vis* Iraq. Europe would do well therefore to prepare for a proactive role in any event.

Meanwhile, time is not wholly in Europe's favour. A lot of time is needed to train and equip the armed forces of Iraq, and to forge a consensus about a political project that the Iraqi soldiers that are to do the fighting can believe in. Absent that, no matter how lavishly equipped, they will never be a reliable force. Fortunately there have now been some limited military successes on the ground, but as events in Yemen show, the survival of the not very cohesive coalition, loosely bound together only by opposition to IS, is not guaranteed. IS is under pressure, as the increasing rate and brutality of the publicised executions show, but time allows them to consolidate their hold on the territories that they have captured and to continue to lure young Europeans (and others, from as far afield as Australia and South East Asia for example) to their cause. Similarly, the more time goes by the more Assad clings to his remaining hold on power. And as time elapses, Libya is just sinking deeper and deeper into the quagmire. The air campaign, clearly, is a holding operation. But holding for what? If the air campaign is but theatre, deceiving ourselves into believing that we are addressing the problem, it will in the end be counter-productive. If it buys time for the diplomatic offensive that is indispensable for a wider settlement for the region, then its effect will be positive. That part has yet to be scripted, however.

Diplomacy is the way forward. The EU, together with the UN, the US and (in spite of the crisis in Ukraine) Russia, has no option but to keep putting pressure on all parties in Syria to bring them to the negotiating table. In view of the stalemate in the civil war, any agreement may have to include a continued role for Assad, at least in a transitional phase, for it to be workable. However much we may dislike the idea on principle, the crisis in Iraq has probably tilted the balance in favour of pragmatism. A ceasefire between the non-IS opposition and Assad is indeed what the latter has been aiming at by consciously targeting the former and avoiding to attack the IS. But as continued fighting is unlikely to break the stalemate it would only result in more loss of life, while a ceasefire would allow efforts to be focussed on the IS.

The attempt to involve Iran in the Syrian negotiations was very wise and has to be kept up. A settlement for Syria has to take into account the proxy war with Saudi Arabia that is going on. The EU's role is not to take sides in this quest for regional dominance, but to strive for a regional arrangement in which all find their place, hence the strategic importance of the broader negotiations with Iran itself. Care must be taken not to jeopardize the outcome of these by appearing so eager that Tehran would no longer see a reason to make many concessions – European energy companies especially are chafing at the bit. Ultimately Iran needs to be a part of the political solution that the region requires; a final deal on its nuclear programme is a *preconditio sine qua non*. The preliminary agreement of Lausanne of 2 April 2015 did at last introduce a glimmer of hope. A normalization of relations with Iran would be a breakthrough indeed. Normalization can only go so far, in view of the serious human rights issues in Iran (such as the hanging of homosexuals), though the situation in Saudi Arabia, the West's "ally" in the Gulf is hardly any better. But even a limited shift towards constructive relations on an issue-by-issue basis would be a game-changer for the Middle East and the Gulf – and there probably is a much bigger chance of transition in Iran, which is in many ways a much more open society, than in Saudi Arabia. Europe could thus try to maintain an equidistant position between Riyadh and Tehran, further diversify energy supply, and help stabilize the Middle East. As the US role *vis-à-vis* Iran remains constrained, for domestic political reasons, the EU is best placed to imagine an ambitious diplomatic scheme for the region as a whole.

Hybrid Hysteria

If Europe is to design a sound security policy towards its neighbourhood, it is important that it make a sober assessment of the security situation, one which goes beyond the hype of the day. In Brussels, "hybrid" is replacing "comprehensive" as the favourite container notion of the foreign policy community. They might not be so different, in fact. Both a hybrid and a comprehensive approach mean the integrated use of a broad range of instruments of external action towards the achievement of a foreign policy objective. It is just that the hybrid approach put into practice by Russia today seeks to achieve rather less friendly aims than the EU's own comprehensive approach. The hybrid approach is the comprehensive approach gone over to the dark side of the force.

But before we get all hysterical over so-called hybrid threats, which are usually associated with Russia, it is essential that we define what we are talking about. Only then can the EU decide if and how its strategy needs to be adapted.

The most eye-catching hybrid approach is *hybrid warfare* as practiced by Russia in Ukraine: fomenting armed rebellion by covert (or at least officially denied) arms deliveries, troop contributions and military operations, propping up friendly local leaders, propaganda, promises of economic benefits and threats of economic reprisals. The aim can be regime change or secession of part of the territory (which can then quickly become a puppet state). Whether the method (the warfare) be hybrid or covert or not: the key thing is that this is war.

One step down from war is *subversion*, which is what many fear is happening in the Baltic states: fomenting political unrest by all means short of military action on the ground, but including for example cyber-attacks, incursions into national airspace and territorial waters, espionage, corrupting politicians and other opinion-makers, propaganda, and economic sticks and carrots. The aim is to turn part of the population against the regime so as to weaken it and render it less able to exercise its sovereignty, including in foreign policy. Staying below the threshold of clear armed aggression, subversion blurs the boundaries of what constitutes an attack that would trigger an armed response or the activation of a collective defence commitment such as NATO's Article 5. Thus the target governments and its allies are kept off-balance.

Covert wars and active subversion are obviously violations of national sovereignty and therefore illegal under international law. Because today this is happening in Europe, it makes us nervous, but we seem to have forgotten to which extent we have engaged in this ourselves in other parts of the world. Many regimes in Latin America, Africa and Asia were subverted or brought down and replaced by a leader judged more amenable by the West during the Cold War and – let's not kid ourselves – even afterwards. This is not to justify Russia's actions in any way, but to put them into perspective. These are not dark new powers that Russia is displaying, but time-honed tactics. Alarmism is not just unnecessary; it is also singularly unhelpful.

For one, it has led commentators to apply the adjective "hybrid" far too widely, to any action aimed at gaining influence within the EU and NATO. Attempting to play off one Member State against another, sponsoring Euro-sceptic and Russia-friendly political parties and NGOs, buying space to spread their message in the media, investing in critical infrastructure, promising financial aid to vulnerable governments, instrumentalizing the energy trade, even military posturing: we may not like it when Russia does this, but these are normal instruments of statecraft. Some of their uses may be reprehensible, but they are certainly not illegal. Are we not regularly using the same levers of power? Europe funds and supports political dissidents and human rights activists across the world, promotes democratization (which in many countries really means regime change), and instrumentalizes its economic power through political conditionality. Of course, EU objectives are not as malicious as those of Russia *vis-à-vis* Ukraine, at least not in its own mind. How they are perceived by some in the target states is another matter. Europeans are just no longer used, since the Cold War ended, to be on the receiving end themselves.

Furthermore, hybrid warfare, subversion and gaining influence are all instruments of statecraft, just like – for good or for bad – terrorism, aerial bombardment and invasion are instruments. And one does not adopt strategies aimed exclusively at an instrument – one makes strategies tailored to the actors that might use those instruments. Countering hybrid threats is as meaningless as an organizing principle of grand strategy therefore as declaring war on terrorism is, if not more so, given the range of activities that hybrid threats can cover. Some general counter-measures must of course be taken: if one fears aerial bombardment, one invests in air defences and shelters; if cyber-attacks are a likely threat, then one builds up one's cyber defences. But this reactive component ought not to be the main part of Europe's strategy for its neighbourhood. The major, proactive part of strategy ought to aim at changing the behaviour of the actor that might undertake bombardment or cyber-attacks. Who that actor is determines how and when these instruments may be used against us and how likely that is.

Which measures should Europe then take?

As stated already, the risk of war, hybrid or otherwise, against an EU/NATO Member State remains very small. What about subversion? For an outside actor to subvert part of a population of a state there have to be pre-existing grievances of sufficient severity against that state, as well as an affinity (cultural, linguistic, historical, political) with the external actor, which has to offer a credible and attractive alternative project. In other words, before subversion is possible, there has to be a domestic political failure. These conditions are clearly present in Ukraine, which has been divided for years between a European and a Russian-oriented public, and where the government has not managed to provide equally for the security, freedom and prosperity of all citizens. Why would anyone think similar Russian subversion would be feasible anywhere else in the EU? What attractive narrative could Russia possibly offer to an EU citizen – as long as the EU and its Member States uphold our social model that ensures that everybody does indeed feel respected, and provided for, as a citizen? The only exception could be the Russian minorities in the Baltic states, which is why the EU should help these three governments to fully integrate all of their citizens in the polity, politically, socially and economically.

A much greater threat, which has already materialized, is subversion by jihadist extremists, who convince EU citizens to join their ranks and go and fight in Iraq and Syria, and to commit acts of terrorism in their home countries in Europe. This has been possible precisely because sizeable proportions of our citizens with an immigrant background feel greatly disenchanted with our society, which it is felt has relegated them to the margins. The greater their despair with their future in Europe, the more attractive the IS narrative becomes, offering adventure, prosperity or salvation – whatever the prospective recruit is most longing for (Coolsaet, 2015). The only safeguard against such subversion is to make sure that Europe's social model does not leave anybody behind, and to ensure that all citizens' security is protected, their voice heard in democratic decision-making, their human rights respected, their equal treatment before the law guaranteed, and, most importantly, that all citizens can enjoy what they perceive as a fair share of the prosperity that our societies produce. The first line of defence against subversion could be said to be Commission President Juncker's investment plan therefore.

Finally, the EU can take measures to reduce its vulnerability and to prevent outside actors (not only Russia, but including China and others) from gaining undue political influence. Obvious measures include increasing cyber defences and the security of critical infrastructure. Another set of measures that is already in the making concerns diversifying energy supply while integrating European energy markets, thus reducing the opportunity for energy blackmail. A new area in which EU policy is called for is oversight of foreign investment in sensitive sectors (banking, energy, transport, telecommunications, and, very importantly, the media). While there is no harm in a company from one EU Member State controlling major shares of such sectors in another, the EU ought to adopt legislation to limit the degree of control that can be exercised by any foreign actor (private or public), from Russia, China, or elsewhere (In the case of the media, one is tempted to explicitly mention Australia). A fourth area is anti-corruption, at the European and national level. Has the time not come for a harmonization across the EU of the rules that govern the funding of political parties?

An area in which the EU should not venture, is propaganda. So-called strategic communications are important: governments must explain to their own citizens what they are doing and why. When they intervene in another country (diplomatically, economically, militarily) they should communicate with citizens there as well. If a certain population is specifically targeted by a propaganda campaign by a foreign actor, or a foreign-funded internal actor, a specific counter-narrative can be developed and a public diplomacy campaign launched. But all of this is something else than propaganda, because a democracy ultimately deserves truth. That is why if the EU does what it should do and does it well, free media will convey that much more effectively and credibly than any government-owned media outlet will ever be able to.

An EU that would consolidate its internal cohesion and reduce its vulnerability to malevolent external actors through what, if one wants, can be called a "counter-hybrid" strategy, would be much better placed to design and implement the external strategies that it really needs: a Russia strategy, a Middle East strategy, etc. Ultimately, one cannot make strategy against an adjective.

A Newly Packaged Neighbourhood Policy

If the security situation can at least be kept under control, the EU can revitalize its long-term multilateral and bilateral relations with the countries in its broader neighbourhood.

If the basic idea of its grand strategy, that well-governed democracies are the key to keeping the peace in its neighbourhood, still holds true, Europe does require new regional strategies on how to bring this grand strategy into practice. Strategies, plural: the notion that a single Neighbourhood Policy can fit all of Europe's neighbours has been proved wrong. The dynamics in the east (geographically and culturally in Europe, but also within the ambit of a power with irredentist designs, Russia) and the south (in Africa and Asia, where multiple powers compete for influence) are just too different. At the same time, the EU has come to realize that "the neighbours of the neighbours" are often as crucial to its interests. In reality therefore, at least five partially overlapping and strongly interrelated areas are of vital importance to European security: the eastern neighbourhood, the Mediterranean, the Sahel, the Horn of Africa, and the Middle East/Gulf. Each of these requires its own sub-regional strategy and multilateral forum as a framework for bilateral relations.

In diplomacy, symbols matter. The EU would do well to gradually phase out the ENP brand, which rightly or wrongly has become associated with failure, in favour of an Eastern, Mediterranean, Sahel, Horn of Africa and Middle Eastern/Gulf strategy. The four southern areas could still be framed in one overarching concept, but the emphasis should be on the sub-regional strategies. These should be issue-based and thus geographically overlapping. The EU has a tendency, manifest also in the ENP, to see the world through the artificial geographic divides that are but its own creation and do not always reflect reality on the ground. Different issues generate different regional dynamics, hence the EU should be flexible and approach the same country in the context of different regional policies according to the issue at hand. If on one issue it makes sense to have e.g. Algeria and Jordan around the same table, on other issues one needs to convene Algeria and Mali while Jordan would have but little interest. Such a flexible approach of course requires prioritization and strong coordination between the five regional policies, in order to avoid that neighbouring countries would be confronted with contradictory expectations.

A multilateral forum for each region adds value to the bilateral relations, at least as a confidence and security-building measure, for the countries of each of the five regions often are embroiled in tensions and disputes among themselves. Multilateralism can also help to foster cooperation between sets of countries on concrete issues. The more operational the multilateral forums can be the better therefore, which requires a focussed agenda. That certainly holds true for the two existing forums: the Eastern Partnership and the Union for the Mediterranean, which have both suffered from "summitry": too many meetings without clear deliverables. Multilateral relations with the Gulf countries, via the Gulf Cooperation Council (GCC), need to become much more political. For the Sahel and the Horn, European security initiatives in these regions can be the starting point for less institutionalized but focussed multilateral meetings. In addition, ad hoc meetings in various constellations can be envisaged, including Iran, in function of the issue to be addressed.

Within this revamped multilateral approach, an equally new way of conducting bilateral relations could then be launched.

The first changes were announced already in the spring of 2011 and were aimed at the southern neighbourhood, in reaction to the Arab Spring. But this initial EU response was a classic example of the programmatic approach to foreign policy: heavy on process and short on politics. Under the heading of "More for More", extra means were allocated in order to provide more support (the "three Ms": money, mobility, and market access), on a differentiated basis, to the countries in the southern neighbourhood that undertake more reforms. This reads like an exact summary of the method of positive conditionality envisaged by the ENP when it was launched in 2004. How is "more of the same" going to make a difference? Some extra money was mobilized: €1.2 billion on top of €5.1 billion for the years 2011–2013. A proposed structural 40 per cent increase for the ENP-budget to €18.1 billion for the budgetary period 2014–2020 fell through however; the European Neighbourhood Instrument now has €15.4 billion available for all 16 eastern and southern neighbours together. That is a considerable amount and such sums can only be generated at the EU level, not by individual Member States. But between €100 and €200 million per country per year: that is not of an order of magnitude that will allow the EU to determine the future of a country like Egypt. The scale of the problem simply is too large, and of course other players are active as well, including some with more resources. Besides, all these figures pale in comparison to the €300 billion that the EU through various mechanisms has committed to bail out Member States since the financial crisis hit us in 2008. More importantly, more budget will not produce more results if the policy that it funds itself continues unaltered. But in spite of the meagre results of the policy and of all the changes in the region, the EU at first remained very reluctant to fundamentally review the ENP.

But Europe cannot continue to make policy *for* rather than *with* its southern neighbours. In reality, the conditionality approach of the ENP is about paternalism rather than partnership: if a country behaves well, it receives a reward from the EU. As we have seen, this approach has worked in the eastern neighbourhood where, because of historical reasons, people can naturally connect more easily with Europe than people in the south. Less than in Cold War Poland perhaps but much more than in present-day Egypt, people in Ukraine can think in terms of a return to Europe and a restoration of the freedom which they briefly enjoyed and was then taken away from them. In the south however, history inevitably leads people to see Europe not just as paternalist, but as foreign, neo-colonial and neo-imperialist and therefore conditionality fundamentally limits the attractiveness of the EU here. As Isaiah Berlin (1998) notes, paternalism:

> is an insult to my conception of myself as a human being; any individual might", he supposed, "prefer to be bullied and misgoverned by some member of my own race or class, by whom I am, nevertheless, recognized as a man and a rival – that is as an equal – to being well and tolerably treated by someone from some higher and remoter group, someone who does not recognize me for what I wish to feel myself to be (p. 228).

Even if the EU would suddenly start implementing the ENP as originally intended, which as we saw it never did and which is unlikely to happen now, Brussels would do better to accept that conditionality will not work in a part of the globe where whatever is emanating from the former colonial powers will be seen as suspect. People in Tunisia, Egypt and Libya courageously rose up in a genuine popular movement against oppressive regimes, at great peril to their lives, to recover their dignity. Simply embracing a foreign model (from Europe, Turkey, the Gulf or elsewhere) is felt to jeopardize that dignity once more, especially as their own history and culture offer a rich source of inspiration to legitimize a new regime of their own. Fortunately that means that other outside powers that are also in "the game" in Europe's southern neighbourhood (the Gulf States, Russia, China) find it is not a walk-over either. But they are intent on gaining influence and they are on the rise.

Europe should rejoice in this popular awareness, for the revolutions in Tunisia, Egypt and Libya do in effect prove the universality of the aspiration to equality in terms of security, freedom and prosperity. That people have become citizens, actively participating in politics, voicing their priorities and concerns, and protesting when their rights are violated, is the most effective safeguard against a return to authoritarianism. In Marxist terms, people (or a new generation of people) have discovered their class consciousness, and once that happens the genie cannot be put back into the bottle. The results are not guaranteed: in Egypt, mass protest against the policies of newly elected President Mohamed Morsi, from the Muslim Brotherhood, led to a military coup and the reinstallation of a military regime under Field-Marshal (now President) Abdel Fattah el-Sisi (July 2013) rather than to more democracy. The Arab Spring has thus just led to the replacement of one general by another. But in Tunisia, for example, the democratic action of the people forced all parties to adopt the language of democracy and human rights and to work towards a relief of their true concerns. Because of linguistic and cultural links, this is a region-wide development across the Arab world. Simultaneously, the Maidan movement in Ukraine has repercussions throughout the eastern neighbourhood, and in some way has given hope to dissidents in the remaining authoritarian regimes in Europe – though the Russian intervention also gives them cause for concern.

Far from leading the EU to abandon its value-based grand strategy, the Arab Spring should thus bring it to reconfirm it – but in the full realization that the tactics must change. Outside Europe, short of invasion and regime-change, outside intervention will not deliver sweeping change, as the ENP vainly promised. A more equal society cannot be mechanically engineered from the outside, by sticks and carrots. It can only emerge as the result of a genuine domestic movement, which external actors cannot create, but can help to foster, support and consolidate, as long as the local actors perceive that they control events and not the foreign well-wisher, no matter how benevolent.

Finally in 2015 the EU did come to realize that a real review of its ENP was necessary. The Commission published a joint consultation paper, thus admitting implicitly that "More for More" was not enough, and this time asked the fundamental questions, starting with: "Should the ENP be maintained?" (European Commission, 2015, p. 4). In the east, the EU can continue the ENP more or less along the existing lines, with association and free trade as objectives; EU membership is not now in the cards. The big question is: how far east does the logic of conditionality apply? Is it appealing to all of the Caucasus countries? In the south a very different ENP is in any case required. The question should also be asked whether Central Asia could and should be targeted by such a new ENP, adding an additional sub-region to it. At heart, the following three principles apply to both east and south.

First, before programmes and projects comes classic diplomacy: to engage with all actors on the political scene, as the EEAS has begun to do, permanently and incessantly, to create mutual understanding and to reinforce the climate in which a democratic and human rights discourse appears natural and inevitable. This will of course be easier in countries where politics have been unfrozen and democracy is being established (such as Tunisia and Mali), but should also be done in countries that are still in transition and the outcome uncertain (such as Libya), or where no coloured revolution or Arab Spring arrived at all (such as Algeria). Even in the latter group of countries, more or less authoritarian regimes feel compelled to take into account public opinion more than before for fear of their own security. In all of these countries the EU should speak with everybody who is in power and with everybody in the opposition. Whether actors are likeable or not is not an issue – what counts is that they are actors.

That includes religiously inspired actors. Seen from secular Europe, the rising role of religion in politics (not just in the Arab world but also in the US, by the way) understandably and justifiably causes concern. In a region where religion plays a pervasive role in public life it should not have come as a surprise though. The secular, western-oriented groups that Europeans and Americans like to talk to usually command but marginal domestic influence. "Political Islam" comes in many guises, but if the Arab Spring produces a Muslim-Democracy, Europe, where Christian-Democracy provided the first President of the European Council, Herman Van Rompuy, and the Chancellor of the largest Member State, Angela Merkel, ought to welcome it. Treating the new incumbents in countries like Tunisia as a political family like any other while they acquire the experience of governing, a priori there is no reason why the normal political cycle of majority and opposition should not apply, in the face of a public opinion concerned first and foremost with political and economic equality.

Second, Europe has a lot of technical expertise that it can offer in pursuit of its foreign policy objectives. Reform of the justice and security apparatus (and the legal framework), adapting it to serve a democratic polity where that exists, is of evident importance. But even in authoritarian regimes promoting good governance and anti-corruption in for example customs and the judiciary can be means of influence. The EU has plenty of experience in deploying its judges, police officers, customs officials, civil protection experts and other civil servants abroad to help other countries. Another priority area is the media: training and exchanges can help consolidate free media and dispel the temptation to over-regulation in the face of an extremely varied and lively and therefore not invariably responsible post-censorship media landscape in newly emerged democracies. Private investment in the media sector by European groups could help ensure independence and plurality. The key is that expertise should be offered, but not imposed, for that would minimize its impact. The country concerned should at all times have the feeling that it is in control. Even when the EU rightly feels that a government needs more support than it is willing to admit and should act more resolutely, as was the case of border security in Libya, the interests of that government will eventually lead it to decisions.

Where the willingness to accept an offer of support exists, the EU should grasp it and be more generous with personnel, equipment, and funds as well as ambitious qua objectives. A few dozen advisors alone will not help much to assure Libya's border security, to refer to that example again. Unfortunately, it remains a struggle to find sufficient civilian "capabilities" to deploy. The reason is simple: unlike the armed forces, whose sole duty it is (next to territorial defence, of course) to prepare for operations abroad, judges and police officers for example are all "deployed" full-time on the EU Member States' own territory. Every European judge sent to Kosovo is one judge less to work on the backlog of cases at home. Every police officer sent to Afghanistan is one less officer to patrol the streets at home. Given the huge demand for civilian experts, part of the solution could be to hire a number of people at the EU level, who would then always be available for deployment abroad.

Third, the biggest challenge that all southern neighbours face is the economic one: how to provide a fair share of prosperity to all members of surging populations? The region has seen little real economic development, due in no small part to an absence of investment, certainly not in export-oriented sectors. The ENP has created an elaborate legal framework to facilitate foreign investment, but far too little use has been made of it by European firms, especially when compared with the Gulf States. On the one hand, this is not to wonder given rampant corruption and crony capitalism in many parts of the region. Yet it is striking that in an era of delocalization of European firms, too few have opted to invest in the Middle East or North Africa; a great many have gone eastwards, to Asia. At least since 1995, when the Barcelona Conference launched the Euro-Mediterranean Partnership (the predecessor of the ENP in the south), the EU has sunk large amounts of money in its southern neighbourhood. What has it got to show for it? Which durable effects has this produced?

Less than a mere lack of money, the issue is how the money is spent. EU funds are best allocated to generate more funds, from Europe's private sector (including through private-public partnerships) and from international players, to invest in the region. Major infrastructure projects, notably in transport and (renewable) energy are particularly promising and will benefit Europe and the region alike. This requires efforts at EU and Member State level: channelling private investment to the region is something that once the EU has created the framework only national governments can really do. In order to attract investors, establishing the rule of law and halting corruption, at least where foreign investments are concerned, are indispensable; perhaps the Asian experience with special economic zones can be helpful in this regard. Key is that investment is linked to a fairer distribution of the wealth that it generates, so as to increase equality in the target country. By offering higher wages, social services, schooling and so on to employees, such projects have an important exemplary role to play.

Because the previous geographic boundaries of the southern ENP no longer make sense, if they ever did, the same bilateral relationship can be aimed at with all countries of all four southern sub-regions, in the Mediterranean, the Sahel, the Horn, and the Middle East/Gulf. There is no reason why Mali would not be offered the same opportunities for close relations with Europe as Tunisia; the stability of both countries is important to safeguard European interests. A really tailor-made approach to the bilateral relationship that at the same time would leave more choice to the neighbouring country, and would thus make for a more equitable relationship with the EU, is now being mentioned in Brussels: offering various issue-based packages of cooperation and support to Europe's neighbours, from which they could choose at their own discretion and agree a mutually beneficial range of activities with the EU. This would give more ownership to the neighbours, while at the same time leaving the EU more freedom to focus cooperation on its own interests. Packages could cover human rights, democracy, security sector reform, mobility of people, transport, energy, etc. but also intelligence, security, and defence.

As stated in the previous chapter: this is first of all about diplomatic relations, not partnership. Therefore all packages could be open to all neighbours, except that the EU should not engage in forms of cooperation that reinforce the authoritarian nature of any regime; cooperation with the security services is particularly sensitive in this regard. Vice versa no package would be imposed upon any neighbour, but if the EU and a neighbour decide to move to real partnership and conclude an association agreement for example, that presupposes a degree of consensus on foreign policy objectives and legitimate ways of achieving them that has to find its expression in a substantial human rights package.

Relations with its neighbours confront Europe with many difficult dilemmas. The European Commission occasionally does put things clearly:

> Our neighbours' strategic orientations determine the extent to which each of them wishes to engage with different actors including the EU. Some partners have chosen to engage on a path of closer association with the EU, and the EU is ready to deepen its relations with them. Others prefer to follow a different path. The EU respects these sovereign choices and is ready to seek other forms of engagement. (2015, p. 3)

On the one hand, after the Arab Spring and the coloured revolutions Europeans feel ill at ease continuing relations with authoritarian regimes. Can the EU carry on as if nothing has happened, condoning the authoritarian traits of one regime while supporting the revolution that has brought down another. On the other hand, given the turmoil the neighbourhood is in already, would it really be wise to actively encourage regime change with the risk of creating even more instability and conflict? Ultimately the fate of any regime depends on its own citizens, not on Europe. The "package approach" allows Europe to engage in diplomatic relations will all states without compromising is own values. Simultaneously the EU can send a strong message that any country that moves towards democratization can move from "packages" to real partnership.

Even within a new ENP, conditionality cannot be entirely abandoned. For both old and new regimes it must be clear that Europe does have red lines when it comes to basic human rights and that if a certain threshold is crossed there will be consequences for the relationship. But this should be an ultimate resort, the system's emergency brake, not its gearbox.

Finally, it seems unlikely that any neighbour will move from partnership to membership of the EU in the near future. That one day all the Balkan states will join the Union is not contentious – they are already surrounded by the EU anyway. It will just take time before they are ready. If ever Iceland, Norway or Switzerland vote to join, they will be welcomed with open arms. But there EU enlargement will probably halt for a long time to come. Whether one is in favour of Turkey's accession or not: it will likely never happen, because the domestic political constellation within the EU that could make it possible will never happen. Would it not be better therefore to give up the pretence, on both sides, and define another type of relationship? Could Turkey not be a strategic partner for example? In the case of Ukraine, the commitment not to apply for EU (and NATO) membership seems advisable in order to reach a durable settlement with Russia. The country would not be ready for decades in any case. Besides, the EU would do better to significantly change its own decision-making machinery before letting in any new members.

Conclusion

As violence and foreign intrusion threaten the stability of many of Europe's neighbours, with full-blooded war going on in several countries when I write these lines, our broader neighbourhood certainly is in the worst state since several years. But that does not mean that Europe is impotent to deal with this. If the EU deploys them pragmatically, its diplomatic, military, civilian and economic instruments, and indeed its values themselves, can have a great impact. The key, as ever, is strategy: setting clear objectives and choosing instruments and allocating means in function of those priorities. In the simplest of terms: not just doing things with the neighbours, but doing things for a purpose.

In this context, the EU has to work with the great powers, simply because they are the great powers. Their non-obstruction, if not their active cooperation, is needed to advance in key areas, notably in Europe's neighbourhood, such as the negotiations about Syria and Iran. Economic ties are way too close and important to permanently put at risk. Tempting though some may find it to revert to Cold War frames, it is imperative to maintain constructive relations with Russia where possible. Issue-based cooperation with all of its "strategic partners", whenever the EU finds that it can agree on the way to protect shared interests, is precisely the way of pulling them into effective and rule-based multilateralism as Brussels sees it.

Whether with neighbours or with the great powers: partnership is not marriage. The EU does not have to declare its love, but it does have to be able to compartmentalize and to proceed on specific issues where possible even while there are major disagreements on other issues at the same time.

Chapter 3

European Defence:
Support your Local Sheriff!

"Cannon to right of them, cannon to left of them, cannon in front of them" (Tennyson, 1854). And is there a collective will and strong leadership behind them? The security situation in Europe's neighbourhood does seem bleak. In the previous chapter we already saw that for the EU's Neighbourhood Policy to be successful, Europe must assume responsibility for security. Is the state of defence in Europe sufficient to that end, to address this challenging geopolitical landscape, in Europe's neighbourhood and beyond? Europeans are muddling through, in NATO, the EU, and ad hoc coalitions, but the downward trend in European defence spending continues. Often Europeans do act with resolve, but never consistently so; they rarely act in unison, and certainly without any overall strategy. Should Europe be concerned?

Ending European Dependence

In the not very distant past most Europeans did not really feel all that responsible for crisis management, for they felt safe in the knowledge that if push came to shove the US would always be there to help them out. It could be said that they saw this as the reward for their subservience to Washington in strategic matters: that even after the end of the Cold War the US would continue to assume responsibility for crisis management in Europe's neighbourhood and provide the bulk of the forces. Of this illusion Europe was quickly disabused however, for when the civil war in Yugoslavia broke out in 1991, the US declared that this was not its fight. And quite right it was, indeed many in Europe felt that this was "the hour of Europe". Yet when it tried to take charge of crisis management itself, Europe failed spectacularly. That only reinforced its dependence on the US, which eventually had to become involved anyway, all the way until the Kosovo war in 1999. Today it is even more obvious that mere subservience is no longer sufficient to secure American support. For sure, American demands for more burden-sharing are as old as NATO itself. But today the US demands a lot more than it used to from its European allies and partners in NATO (which for the US remains the core of the transatlantic relationship, through which it prefers to channel most consultation and cooperation).

The reason is that in the face of the pivot of its own strategy towards Asia, the US seeks to maintain a much more hands-off approach to European security. The US was of course present in Asia before the pivot with large numbers of troops, notably in its bases in Japan and South Korea – numbers which it maintains, while US forces in Europe now consist mostly of those manning the command structures, airfields and depots that serve as hubs for potential deployment further afield. Because the US is a global power with global interests, events will force the US to get involved wherever its interests are threatened, but that does not alter its fundamental strategic calculus: the main challenge is seen to emerge from Asia. Other problems, especially European problems, are seen as distractions that stop the US from focusing on its actual priorities, rather than as priorities in their own right. US officials keep saying to Europeans that what they really meant was not so much a pivot as a rebalancing of American strategic engagements, but this is semantics. The reality is that this is a pivot, and not a pirouette: rather than a constant to and fro it is a structural rebalancing that will not be altered if another party gains the White House. This is so not just because America's eyes are firmly fixed on China, but also because there is a growing feeling of overstretch as the US defence budget is under pressure, massive though it remains compared to everyone else's, and because of the decreasing bond with Europe of many of the political leadership (especially in Congress), and the sense of insufficiency after a series of failed or at most moderately successful interventions. For all these reasons, even when the US does engage around Europe, it does so much more reluctantly than before (Howorth, 2014, p. 142). Of course the US remains committed to collective defence under NATO's Article 5, because the security of Europe's territory is a vital American interest (Michaels, 2014). But it will no longer automatically take the lead in addressing non-Article 5 security issues around Europe that do not directly menace European territory.

Next to the new direction of American strategy and consequent US demands upon Europe, there is an additional dimension to the need for Europeans to leave their subservience behind them and that is that Europeans have less trust in American strategy than before. Not only does the US no longer intervene automatically in every crisis around Europe in order to protect Europe's interests – that was the lesson taught by the Yugoslav wars. When it does intervene, its actions can also go directly against European interests – that was the lesson of the 2003 invasion of Iraq. Until this day the fall-out of the invasion of Iraq is teaching Europe another lesson: that US interventions can fail as spectacularly and disastrously as the European intervention on the Balkans. American interventions have failed before, but Europeans saw the result as "their" problem. This is why until the sudden emergence of IS, Iraq was off the radar screen in Brussels, in both NATO and the EU, hence the surprise when Syria and Iraq suddenly became one theatre of war. Or Europeans considered the problem to be too far from home to really pose a problem for Europe – this is how Europe came to see the war in Afghanistan and how, before, it saw the American defeat in Vietnam. The current crises are very close to home however, and nobody feels confident that the US-led coalition against IS will be successful. Yet somehow Europe will have to deal with the crises around it, with or without the US, either comprehensively and in theatre, or defensively at the borders of Europe. Why? Because European, not American interests are primarily at stake.

The conclusion is that transatlantic burden-sharing no longer only is about putting more European main battle tanks, heavy artillery and conscript battalions into the path of a presumed Soviet invasion. Henceforth the US not only expects Europeans to *contribute* to the Alliance's defences in the east and to US-led crisis management operations. Washington now wants Europeans to *initiate* and lead crisis management themselves. Preferably Europeans would act in an early stage, before a crisis escalates, so that it can still be addressed without overly relying on American assets. American strategy has come full circle, back to the initial plan of the late 1940s: "to get Europe on its feet and off our backs" (Marshall Plan administrator Paul Hoffman, quoted in Brands, 2014, p. 29).

But how have Europeans reacted in reality to the recent crises at their borders? They have asked to be reassured. Ever since the crisis in Ukraine, many eastern European leaders and NATO officials especially have clamoured for visible action in order to prove that Article 5 is to be taken seriously. Read: that the Americans will defend Europe. The higher the clamour is raised, the more it provokes the question: was it not to be taken seriously before then? In NATO surprise seemed to reign at the ability of the Russian military to pull off the deployment in the Crimea, yet one of the assumptions on which NATO defence planning was based was that Russia could not pose a serious threat to the Alliance in less than ten years. Is Europe really as vulnerable as it feels, in spite of being the largest economic bloc and, collectively, the second military power in the world? Advertising a feeling of insecurity hardly seems a sound communications strategy. Should NATO and its members not have confidently stated from the outset, as they eventually did at the Wales Summit in September 2014, that Article 5 was and still is the strongest possible guarantee and that therefore Europe's own territory is secure (NATO, 2014)? Which it is, for the Russian armed forces as a whole are no party for NATO precisely because the Americans will indeed defend us if ever it comes to Article 5. Deterrence works. Europeans therefore ought to have addressed the crisis with much more self-assurance and resolution from the start.

To say that Europe should feel less surprised and less vulnerable is anything but a call for complacency. It is a strong plea for Europeans to get rid of the mind-set of dependence, subservience, and reassurance, which is at the heart of their complacency about defence: why bother, if the US cavalry will come anyway? Instead Europeans have to take charge of stabilizing their neighbourhood themselves. If European defence is but a shop window, Europeans have no choice but to shop in the *stock américain* – which may soon be closing down.

NATO can of course provide reassurance, which was given substance in Wales by the creation of a Very High Readiness Joint Task Force (VJTF) of brigade strength within the existing 21,000-strong NATO Response Force (NRF) – though this is also an implicit admission that the NRF itself is insufficiently responsive. This VJTF is to be on stand-by and to rotate through bases in eastern Europe where supplies and equipment will be pre-positioned. But reassurance does not in itself solve any crisis. In Ukraine crisis management is a matter of diplomacy and sanctions (and low oil prices), which *vis-à-vis* Russia Europeans can only lever through the collective weight of the EU. One positive consequence is that in Washington, NATO headquarters and European capitals it is now widely accepted that there is only one European security architecture, and that all of its component parts are vital to deliver the vaunted comprehensive approach to crisis management: NATO, the EU, and their Member States. The implications of this recognition go much further than the need to align the EU's trade and diplomacy with NATO's military instruments. A new division of labour is emerging (Shea, 2013). Thanks to Putin's meddling in Ukraine, NATO, which was dreading a loss of direction after the drawdown of the operation in Afghanistan, has found a renewed sense of purpose – in a renewed focus on Article 5. The NATO machinery in Brussels focuses very strongly on collective defence. The VJTF for example is mostly seen as an Article 5 measure, which means that while on stand-by these troops can be used exclusively for collective defence. Consequently, crisis management in *all* of its dimensions (diplomatic, economic, and military) will increasingly have to be politically initiated by Europeans – and thus by the EU.

A US where restraint is likely to be the order of the day (Posen, 2014) would actually welcome such a development. The interventions in Libya in 2011 and in Mali in 2013 already were European, though not EU, initiatives. So far however Europe has neither consistently followed up these interventions in order to consolidate their effect (as in Libya) nor consistently initiated responses to all crises in its neighbourhood (as in Syria). A pragmatic review of the state of defence in Europe must make sure that Europe next to its diplomatic and economic power has the military capacity to assume this comprehensive crisis management role.

The Political Ambition: Defining European Responsibilities

But which role exactly do Europeans want to play? The state of defence in Europe can only be assessed relative to the security responsibilities that Europe has the ambition to assume. Alas, that is precisely where there is a huge gap in European strategic thinking.

This gap is not obvious, because it is masked by elaborate (and laborious) defence planning processes and various capability initiatives at the national, NATO and EU level. Through the NATO Defence Planning Process (NDPP), the NATO Strategic Concept and the military level of ambition that results from it (how many operations of which type should the Alliance be capable of?) is translated into a desired capability mix for the Alliance as a whole and in turn into specific capability targets for each individual ally. The question that the NDPP does not answer is what the "European bloc", i.e. the European allies and partners within NATO/the EU Member States, ought to be capable of autonomously, without capabilities from the US (and the other non-European allies). That question has become crucial, because it is increasingly likely that in non-Article 5 contingencies crisis management around Europe will not be undertaken by the Alliance as a whole but by coalitions of Europeans. NATO's defence planning thus prepares Europe for the scenario that for crisis management is the least likely.

Furthermore, once the targets have been set and capability development has to start, no significant additional capabilities will be generated by individual European countries, for they no longer have the scale and the means. This holds true for strategic enablers especially: assets such as long-range transport aircraft, air-to-air refuelling, drones, satellites, and precision-guided munitions that make rapid and precise action at far distances possible. All of these require such large means that they can only be afforded by pooling European efforts. It is exactly in strategic enablers that Europe is most deficient: Europeans can still muster sizeable numbers of fighter aircraft and infantry battalions, but there is no point in having those if you cannot keep them in the air for lack of air-to-air refuelling, or cannot field them where they are needed in the absence of strategic transport. Everybody knows that Europe needs more air-to-air refuelling capacity for example – but to be able to do what exactly? Air policing in the Baltics? Bombing Libya? Bombing IS? Without an indication of the political level of ambition it is impossible to quantify how much capability exactly Europe requires and to design the right mix that would allow Europeans to act alone if and when necessary.

Who is to provide the answer to the question which autonomous role Europe wants to play as a security provider?
The answer cannot be derived from the NATO Strategic Concept, because this is a foreign policy question, first of all, and not just a defence issue. Which security commitment Europe needs to assume in its broader neighbourhood, for example, depends on which political and economic relations Europe aspires to with its neighbours. If and when Europeans seek to answer that type of foreign policy questions collectively, they do so through the EU. The best placed therefore to adopt a formal level of ambition for Europe is the European Council: an intergovernmental body where the EU heads of state and government take decisions by unanimity. Surely they, if anybody, can lend real political weight to a statement of ambition that European states will subsequently regard as a guideline for their defence efforts in both NATO and the EU. This is more politically feasible than it may appear. In a report preparing its December 2013 meeting for which European Council President Herman Van Rompuy had put "the state of defence in Europe" on the agenda, Ashton as High Representative put forward an unexpectedly frank formulation of Europe's ambitions.

What did Ashton's report say? Europe needs strategic autonomy. Read: Europe needs to be able to act without the US if necessary. That applies first of all to our broad neighbourhood, the report added. As we have seen in chapter 2, everybody has come to agree that Europe's "real" neighbourhood, the area where its interests are directly at stake, is larger than the area covered by the Neighbourhood Policy. Ashton's report explicitly stated that it includes the "neighbours of the neighbours" in the Sahel and the Horn of Africa, and this is where Europeans are effectively deploying. As said in the previous chapter, one should add the Gulf region, for the security of the Middle East is inextricably tied up with that of Iran, Iraq and Saudi Arabia. Less clear is how far the "real" neighbourhood extends to the east. Does it really include the Caucasus? Or does it stretch as far as Central Asia? In this broad neighbourhood, Ashton went on to say, Europeans must be capable of "power projection" to defend their interests, with partners from the region whenever possible but alone if necessary. This was certainly the first time that the notion of power projection was introduced into an EU document, and that by Ashton, who was not known for her interest in military matters, to say the least. Even more surprisingly, this report elicited little or no negative reaction from the capitals (Ashton, 2013). Unfortunately domestic politics got in the way. Just the weekend before the meeting the British tabloid press once again raised the spectre of a "European army" and François Hollande chose this moment to voice the idea that the EU could foot the bill for the French intervention in the Central African Republic, leading David Cameron to a last-moment attempt to scuttle the European Council's defence agenda in its entirety. In the resulting compromise the European Council avoided the strategic discussion and focussed on capabilities and industry. As a preparatory document for a European Council that is now behind us, the report has no formal status.

Ashton's report can be read together however with the EU's Maritime Security Strategy, adopted in 2014, which looks beyond the neighbourhood and renders explicit Europe's interest in global maritime security, without spelling out though whether this implies a global naval role in addition to Europe's leading role in anti-piracy operations off the coasts of Africa (Council of the EU, 2014a). Finally, there is the fact that Europeans, in line with the 2003 European Security Strategy, continue to promote the collective security system of the United Nations as a central part of the global order. Europe assumes responsibilities in that context as well, as witnessed by the deployment of an EU operation in the Central African Republic in 2014 (following up on a French intervention) as well as by contributions from several EU Member States to UN blue helmet operations.

From the practice of operations initiated and led by Europeans (under the EU, NATO or national flag) and, increasingly, from the EU discourse, a three-tiered set of security responsibilities is thus emerging:

1. Assuming first-line responsibility for stabilizing Europe's own broad neighbourhood, including at sea, initiating the comprehensive response (diplomatic, economic and military) to any crisis.
2. Contributing to global maritime security.
3. Contributing to the UN collective security system.

What do these Responsibilities Imply?

The neighbourhood: Inter-state war, including spill-over of a civil war into neighbouring countries, must certainly always be prevented or ended. In such a scenario, the UN Security Council is more likely (though not guaranteed) to seize the matter, and Europe will then probably act as part of a broader coalition, notably with the US, and preferably always with regional actors – but alone if it is the only option. In any scenario a major contribution will be expected. Intra-state conflict, particularly when the Responsibility to Protect arises (in case of war crimes, crimes against humanity, genocide or ethnic cleansing), would ideally be addressed by regional actors. The will and certainly the means to do so remain limited however, hence European intervention will often prove necessary. In such cases, Europe is more likely to be the only or certainly the leading external actor, preferably still in coalition with regional actors, as in Libya and Mali. Unless the government of the country in question requests intervention, a UNSC mandate is much less certain. As in Syria, but also in Georgia (2008), the military feasibility may be constrained by the implication of external powers, the chance that any benefits are outweighed by major negative side effects, or an unacceptably high risk of casualties. Intervention may then be limited to preventing spill-over and possibly supporting the legitimate party in the conflict. Whether it intervened or not, Europe definitely has a responsibility to stabilize any post-conflict situation, including through peacekeeping, SSR/ DDR, and training and assisting local armed forces (as well as the security and justice apparatus).

Maritime security: The ESS states that "in an era of globalisation, distant threats may be as much a concern as those that are near at hand". The most direct as well as most likely threat of force to their vital interests that Europeans face is a disruption of maritime trade (which accounts for 90 per cent of Europe's trade overall). Maritime security is most commonly associated with piracy in the Gulf of Aden, but obviously the very same trade route can also be threatened anywhere between there and the ports of China, and that would be equally problematic. Europeans thus have a vital interest in maritime security in Asia, as well as in other parts of the globe such as West Africa. Furthermore, Somali piracy has demonstrated that maritime problems are rarely solved at sea only. That does not just hold true for the threat of piracy (which is present in Asia and West Africa too). The other main threat to maritime security in Asia is a function of the tensions between China and its neighbours – which clearly calls for more than gunboat diplomacy.

A commitment to maintaining global maritime security thus has far-reaching implications. It is beyond Europe's means to play a leading role in maritime security worldwide, but it should take the lead in addressing maritime issues in its broader neighbourhood and adjacent zones. Europeans have proven themselves able to deal with non-state actors, the most likely threat, like in the case of Somalia, though success still requires a broad international and regional coalition. Europe is well-placed to forge such coalitions, and to initiate the broader comprehensive strategy that is required to address the underlying causes of piracy. Less likely but dramatic if it would materialize is a blockage of the main artery of the Suez canal as a consequence of inter or intra-state war (EUISS, 2013). That too would likely be a crisis which the UNSC would seize and upon which an international coalition would act, of which Europeans would have to be a major part. In Asia, local and regional actors should be counted upon to tackle problems of piracy, but a European contribution would demonstrate how serious the international community takes the issue, thus adding to the credibility and effectiveness of the effort. Moreover, a small but significant permanent naval presence, engaging in exchanges, training, manoeuvres, and patrolling with regional partners and promoting multinational cooperation between them, including China, would constitute an important confidence and security-building measure and contribute to diluting tensions between competing powers. Such a distinctive European naval presence would complement wider European diplomatic efforts at conflict prevention, multilateral dialogue and region-building, and would be much more effective than adding the odd European ship to the American fleet – the 7th Fleet does not need reinforcement. In the Arctic, finally, the main issue is maritime safety rather than security. Here too, Europeans by being present themselves can promote multinational cooperation between the various other actors with a stake in the region.

UN collective security: Given the volatility of their own near abroad, chances are that Europeans' appetite and means to engage in crisis management elsewhere will be limited. Yet, Europe cannot ignore crisis and suffering in other parts of the globe. At first sight its own vital interests may be less directly at stake in conflicts in Sub-Sahara Africa for example, but abidance by the fundamentals of international law (the non-use of force and respect for human rights) is a vital interest as such. Without a general climate of abidance by international law, there can be no international stability and thus no flourishing international trade, nor multilateral cooperation on pressing global challenges. Such a climate can only be upheld when international law is upheld and gross infringements are consistently acted upon. "The United Nations Security Council has the primary responsibility for the maintenance of international peace and security", states the ESS, adding immediately that "Strengthening the United Nations, equipping it to fulfil its responsibilities and to act effectively, is a European priority". For indeed, not only are two of the permanent members of the UNSC European, Europeans need an effective UN in case of crisis in their own near abroad. Would Europeans have intervened in Libya in 2011 without a UN mandate? If they had, the lack of a mandate would certainly have complicated things, as it did in June 2015 when the EU launched a naval operation in the Mediterranean to stop human trafficking. In the absence of a UN mandate or consent from the Libyan government, at the outset the operation had to be limited to international waters and could not enter Libyan territorial waters, let alone target smugglers' installations on shore. The UN can only be effective however if it is perceived to be effective generally, and not just in contingencies in which the interests of the permanent members are directly at stake.

Europeans have a responsibility therefore to contribute to the UN collective security system. That contribution need not just be counted in European blue helmets – at the request of the UN Europeans can deploy under NATO, CSDP or national command, including in support of regional organizations such as the

African Union and ECOWAS – but it cannot be limited to paying into the budget of the Department of Peacekeeping Operations. Europeans cannot and should not contribute to each and every UN (led or requested) operation. Further prioritization within this priority responsibility is needed. R2P can serve as one guideline: having come into being thanks only to a major European diplomatic effort, surely whenever the mechanism is activated Europeans should now also contribute to its implementation. Concentration and consistency of effort could be another guideline. As the case of the Congo illustrates, small-scale operations of fixed duration, even when successful, rarely create durable effects. A small (relative to the overall size of the force) but permanent contribution of European combat forces to the UN operation in the DRC would surely have had a lot more impact than the two short-term CSDP operations in 2003 and 2006, necessary though they were at the time.

What the EU ought to do is to translate this into a formal statement of ambition, to be adopted by the European Council.

Of course, intervention fatigue, a justified preference for non-military solutions and simply lack of unity and resolve mean that Europe is by no means guaranteed to act consistently on these three responsibilities. But the realization is dawning that nobody is likely to assume them instead, not even the US. A formal statement would at least put ongoing engagements in a clear framework, explaining first of all to European publics why Europe is acting. It would also provide guidance for future decision-making on crisis management, helping political leaders to assess when a military response of which nature is necessary and possible. It would further make it clear to Europe's allies, partners, neighbours and others what they can expect from Europe as a contribution to security – and what not. The US would certainly welcome a self-assured statement of which European contribution it can look forward to rather than which reassurance Europeans require. Finally, a formal statement of ambition would be the basis to quantify the capabilities that Europeans need in order to fulfil that ambition autonomously, and would thus provide much-needed guidance for collective European capability development.

The latter is not a call for a new and elaborate defence planning process in the EU, an "EUDPP", alongside the existing NDPP in NATO. Rather it is a plea to complete the NDPP by introducing into it a European level, which it does not now contain, defining which mix of capabilities the European allies and partners as a group require to be capable of autonomous action without the US, so that they can fulfil their ambitions as security providers outside Europe's borders as defined (hopefully) by the European Council. This would take into account the new reality that Europeans have to be able to contribute to collective defence and to participate in US-led crisis management operations and to undertake their own crisis management operations, alone.

Fortunately, the capabilities required for crisis management and collective defence greatly overlap. On the one hand, in most Article 5 scenarios most allies will have to deploy their forces over great distances under severe time constraints, just as for expeditionary crisis management. If NATO's eastern border is threatened, for the Portuguese that is a long-distance deployment. Of course, within NATO territory deployment can to a large extent happen via road and rail instead of by ship and aircraft, and the forces of the allies that are in the threatened area will be in place on their national territory already. On the other hand, heavy firepower is not just required to stop an invader but also for expeditionary land operations, even for peacekeeping before or after a conflict – nothing like a main battle tank to deter a potentially hostile actor. Indeed, conventional deterrence has to enter the dictionary of European strategic thinking again (Simón, 2012). *Vis-à-vis* Russia, first of all: if Russia does not pose a threat to EU and NATO territory it is also because of the military balance between them and the Alliance. But on the NATO side, conventional deterrence relies to far too great an extent on the US. Deterrence will also support European diplomacy in its broader neighbourhood. The availability of a credible European expeditionary force will certainly influence the calculations of Europe's neighbours to both the east and the south. It is a matter of finding the right mix therefore of heavy and light forces, of tactical and strategic transport, to enable Europeans to assume their Article 5 as well as their expeditionary responsibilities. One thing is sure: the transformation of European armed forces must continue. It is a mistake to think that Europeans have in their arsenals some forces capable of high-tech high-end expeditionary operations and other "in place" forces suitable for collective defence. In most cases they have forces capable of expeditionary operations as well as territorial defence and remaining forces that are not very capable at all.

In December 2013 the European Council actually tasked the High Representative and the European Defence Agency (EDA) with putting forward "an appropriate policy framework by the end of 2014, in full coherence with existing NATO planning processes". This sounded very ambitious, but the document that the EU eventually adopted focussed on the operational level of concrete incentives for collaborative programmes rather than on the strategic level of European responsibilities and the required capability mix (Council of the EU, 2014b). Still the question remains unanswered therefore: which role does Europe want to play in security and defence?

One can however already assess the actual state of defence in Europe against the three-tiered set of responsibilities mentioned above that implicitly Europeans do increasingly recognize. For more than a decade now Europeans have sustained the equivalent of a corps (60–70,000 troops) on expeditionary operations, for NATO, EU, UN, national and coalition operations. That is the good news; only the US does better. The bad news is that this is also more or less the maximum that Europeans can do in spite of the fact that they pay well over one and a half million people to wear uniform. The cost effectiveness of its defence effort is very low indeed. For any additional demand, even for manoeuvres on the European continent, as a way of signalling Alliance resolve to Russia, most European nations find themselves scraping the bottom of the barrel. Furthermore, European deployments rely to a very large extent on American enablers (especially ISTAR, air-to-air refuelling, transport, and precision-guided munitions). Even the 2011 air campaign over Libya, immediately adjacent to Europe, could not have been undertaken in the way that it was (maximizing precision, minimizing casualties and collateral damage) without massive US support.

The conclusion is obvious: the state of defence in Europe today does not allow Europeans to play the part that their strategic situation requires. As much was said by Mogherini (2015b, p. 18) herself in the assessment that she presented to the European Council in June 2015: "the current level of ambition and capability targets are not tailored to the strategic environment … and the growing need for Europeans to take responsibility for their own security".

The Military Ambition: Defining European Capability Targets

The solution to this deficit is to step up capability development in Europe, but the first stage must be to review the capability targets, so that Europe gains a detailed picture of what it needs to be capable of autonomous expeditionary action.

The NDPP, as we have seen, simply does not take this into account. The EU itself did define an objective for autonomous action though: the 1999 Helsinki Headline Goal (HHG), adopted by the European Council, aims to sustain a joint engagement adding up to corps strength (50–60,000) for at least one year. This is what Europeans have been doing for more than ten years now, but relying on American enablers, so not autonomously at all. Moreover, if the security situation in the past decade led Europe to permanently deploy the equivalent of the Headline Goal, this proves that as a target it is insufficient, for it leaves Europe without any deployable reserve. Imagine that in 2011 Europeans had decided to deploy ground forces in Libya as well: it would have been very hard to assemble any sizeable number of troops while the majority of well-trained and equipped forces were deployed in Afghanistan or had just returned from a rotation there. In other words, as long as the Headline Goal remains the basis for European capability development, that is severely constrained.

The Headline Goal is translated into detailed capability requirements by the EU Military Staff (EUMS) on the basis of five illustrative scenarios each based on a type of operation that the EU might undertake: peace enforcement, peacekeeping, evacuation of EU citizens, training and assistance to foreign forces, and support to humanitarian relief. But these scenarios have been surpassed by reality too. There is no naval scenario, for example, while Operation Atalanta against Somali pirates has been going on for years. Which capability requirements get priority is then decided through the Capability Development Plan (CDP) that is elaborated by the EDA. The latest, 2014 version of the CDP does go beyond the Headline Goal to some extent (for example in the maritime and cyber area), because it takes into account the results of a questionnaire to Member States about what they see as their national priorities, and the capitals are obviously not bound by the limits of the HHG (European Defence Agency, 2014). The CDP also takes industrial implications into account. If for example Europe wants to maintain a European industry capable of developing drones in the long term, then orders for drones will have to be placed in the short term or the industry will disappear. The CDP process thus allows the EDA to at least try and sketch the full picture, but in the end it has to operate within the boundaries of the Headline Goal, so no capability priorities that go far beyond it can be adopted.

In order to generate capability priorities that correspond to Europe's actual needs, that is to be able to act autonomously upon the triple set of security responsibilities, the very first step would thus have to be the definition of a new Headline Goal. A real and realistic target would be a "double Headline Goal": Europeans ought to be able to undertake up to a corps-sized engagement *over and above* all ongoing operations, and at least in their broad neighbourhood they should be able to do so autonomously, without American enablers. This would be a real objective, for it would provide Europe with the strategic reserve to intervene in a crisis in its own neighbourhood or to deploy to the east as a deterrent in an Article 5 scenario, even when other European forces are already engaged elsewhere. And it would be a realistic objective as well, for set against the 1.5 million people employed by Europe's armed forces even a deployable capacity of two corps would still represent a lower level of cost-effectiveness than the US military (which recently deployed more than 200,000 troops on operations, in addition to those permanently stationed overseas, out of 1.1 million). This revised overall target could then again be translated into detailed capability requirements and priority targets by the EUMS and the EDA, and would thus generate the European level that is to be introduced into the NDPP.

One thing is certain: Europe as a whole will never be able to reach this collective target of deploying up to two corps if individual European countries do not revise their *national* deployability targets upwards. Many countries have recently decreased the numbers that they want to be able to deploy and sustain on operations however. France and Britain now each provide for 6–7,000 troops for ongoing crisis management operations, and some 30,000 for a major enforcement operation (Her Majesty's Government, 2010, pp. 18–19; Ministère de la Défense, 2013, pp. 92–3). Many smaller European countries in their defence white papers talk about battalions or even brigades as the level of manoeuvre units for deployment abroad, but in practice they mostly think in terms of deploying companies. Should not the capacity to deploy at least a battlegroup-size force (one battalion plus support) be within reach of the large majority of European countries? That does not mean that countries have to be able to deploy alone. On the contrary: as we shall see, a combination of pooling and specialization of the support and combat support capabilities and acquiring collective strategic enablers would allow all nations to contribute significant manoeuvre units towards the overall European target. In other words, with a little help of their friends all countries of Europe should be able to field more significant numbers that are deployable and sustainable than they do now. For pooling of efforts to be possible, however, all partners must retain some capabilities worth pooling. Military marriages are traditional: if there is no dowry, there will be no wedding.

For several years now both the EU and NATO have made a persistent effort to promote such pooling and specialization. In December 2011, the EU under Belgian

Presidency launched the Ghent Process, now known as Pooling and Sharing. This seemed so promising that in February 2012 then NATO Secretary-General Anders Fogh Rasmussen went against NATO's own mantra of avoiding duplication between the EU and the Alliance and initiated Smart Defence, which does essentially the same. Fortunately excellent informal staff-to-staff contacts between officials of both organizations have allowed to de-conflict and to some extent coordinate both schemes. One the one hand, both stimulate European nations to join large-scale capability projects that are set up by the EU or NATO themselves in areas where only they can generate the required critical mass, notably to acquire strategic enablers. On the other hand, the EU and NATO promote pooling and specialization between nations in various overlapping regionally or functionally organized clusters of countries. As long as there is no formal statement of ambition for Europe's autonomous security role, all of these ongoing European capability efforts are to some extent hanging up in the air; it is not clear to which capability mix they are meant to contribute. That is not the only reason however why so far progress has been limited.

Capability Development: In Search of an Architect for the Big Projects

NATO has unfortunately not had much success in launching major projects. As a senior official put it to me: the only significant Smart Defence initiatives, those that will increase capabilities, are those that pre-dated the scheme and were subsequently re-branded so that there would be something to show for their efforts. This primarily concerns US-initiated projects that address Alliance-wide capabilities for territorial defence, such as the Alliance Ground Surveillance System (AGS) and missile defence. Most of the other Smart Defence initiatives that NATO has chosen to laud as achievements concern training and pooling of existing capacity: that is welcome and useful, but will not increase capabilities. If it would be going too far to say that this could have been expected, it ought not to come as a total surprise either, because Smart Defence simply goes against the grain of NATO. The NDPP is geared to generate capability targets for each individual nation, hence the Alliance actually does not have much of a track record in multinational capability development, certainly not between Europeans. Indeed, the point of NATO has always been to prevent strong European groupings to emerge, for the more the Europeans in NATO act as a group, the more difficult it is for the US to dominate decision-making. It is also difficult for NATO projects to satisfy both American and European defence industrial interests: the US would like Europe to spend more on defence – and spend by buying American equipment, but of course many European countries want to favour the European defence industry.

Even before the 2014 Wales Summit it was noticeable that Smart Defence was being mentioned less and less in NATO's communication, in favour of the Connected Forces Initiative (CFI). This is a new NATO scheme to maintain the standards of training and interoperability acquired by the experience of operations in Afghanistan by an extensive schedule of manoeuvres. Ever since Wales, the focus is on collective defence and the Readiness Action Plan adopted there, which builds on the CFI, with the VJTF as the most concrete and, at least at first sight, much more feasible objective. As NATO is re-emphasizing Article 5 ever more, which is its exclusive domain, there is a certain risk that coordination with the EU will water down again. Yet in capability development as in strategy both are now inextricably entwined. The VJTF scheme is very useful to enhance the responsiveness of European forces, but it will not itself increase capability. Conclusion: if not through the EU, major capability projects are unlikely to be realized anywhere.

It seems but logical that solving a European capability problem through increased European cooperation is better undertaken through a European organization: the EU. There are of course competing industrial interests among Europeans as well, as the failed BAE-EADS merger in 2012 proves. More and more however the "national champions", defence firms that thrived on their national market alone, are realizing that the scale of national armed forces in Europe has become too small for that model to remain viable. In very few areas are the orders of a single state sufficient to fill the order book. In 2014 even a most traditional firm like Dassault gave up resistance to European cooperation and joined a drone programme with EADS and Finmeccanica. And yet so far progress on the EU side is only marginally better than in NATO. In December 2013 the European Council did somewhat optimistically welcome EDA projects on three strategic enablers, air-to-air refuelling, satellite communication, and drones, as well as on cyber security. By the time of the June 2015 European Council, where defence was again on the agenda, the EDA had achieved progress in making better use of existing capabilities in these four areas and was actively promoting projects to develop new European platforms so as to increase capabilities. But for these projects to take off, more Member States need to participate and they need to invest more money. It is not sufficient, as some Member States do, to send a staff officer to attend every meeting on every project and then to say: we participate.

The main obstacle which blocks large-scale projects in the EU as much as in NATO quite simply is a lack of political will to spend sufficient money on defence. The issue it not so much that more should be spent, but that the continued decline of the defence budgets should be stopped, and that existing budgets should be spend in much more integrated and collective fashion. If they were, the €160 billion that together the 28 EU Member States still devote to defence would be sufficient to provide it with the capabilities required for the triple set of responsibilities that I propose. As long as this is not the case, even increasing defence budgets would be of little help, for pouring more money into a wasteful spending structure just means wasting more money.

As a result of Russia's aggressive behaviour, for the first time in many years European publics may at least question the wisdom of further defence cuts. However, the mantra, incanted once again at the Wales Summit, of spending two per cent of GDP on defence, is a target as unrealistic (for a country like Germany will not double its defence spending) as the language of the Summit declaration is non-committal ("aim to move toward the 2% guidelines within a decade"). Much more important is that allies committed to "halt any decline in defence expenditure" and to devote at least 20 per cent of annual spending to investment. But while some countries have since announced a budget increase, several others, including Britain and France, actually expect more cuts. The next step is to convince countries to spend what money they do have on collective capability projects. This is an uphill struggle: large-scale projects require very large sums, which capitals even if they do invest are always more inclined to spend on national forces than on multinational projects. The latter carry a reputation of always exceeding budgets and never meeting deadlines, which is to some extent deserved. But this should not blind European nations for the harsh reality: few if any of them can still afford big national capability projects. Increasingly, the choice is between investing in multinational European projects and having no projects at all (and thus being obliged to always buy off the shelf from the US).

The key to convincing states to invest in collective European projects is to position the European Defence Agency, which is already the best placed to foster solutions to European shortfalls, even better. The EDA must come to be seen as the indispensable architect of European defence cooperation, which can design tailor-made projects for every need, in the area of strategic enablers as well as any other in which a country seeks partners (Coelmont and Biscop, 2014).

As ever, cost arguments will be the most powerful. Cooperation can drastically reduce not only the cost of development and acquisition of equipment, but also the life-cycle cost of any programme. The starting point is to define a really common configuration for equipment, instead of "gold-plating" it by introducing superfluous national specifications, as happens often today, as a result of which supposedly common equipment is still produced in so many different versions that countries might as well not have cooperated. Once equipment is in use, common updates can be organized as well throughout its entire life-cycle. In addition, permanent common logistics and maintenance can be set up, through pooling and/or specialization between the countries that operate the equipment, to create further savings. If the participants so decide, even the actual use of the capability can be commonly managed. An example that works is European Air Transport Command (EATC), which the December 2013 European Council put forward as a model, which coordinates and optimizes flight movements for the Belgian, Dutch, French, German, Italian, Luxembourg and Spanish transport fleets, to the satisfaction of all involved. The key to achieving maximum cost-efficiency is that the EDA be allowed to act as coordinator throughout a programme's life-cycle: the Agency can chair the common configuration board composed of the states participating in a project; it can act as a single point of contact with the private contractor; it can put forward concrete proposals for cooperation on logistics and maintenance; and it can manage the updates decided upon by the participating states. Just like NATO, such EDA projects can be exempted from VAT.

Funding arguments are crucial as well. If they cooperate on collective projects through the EDA, Member States could be enabled to tap into European resources. The December 2013 European Council consecrated the role of the Commission in defence, notably in research. The Commission was already funding security research, but now defence research will become a permanent fixture of its multi-annual research programmes (such as Horizon 2020) as well. Commission President Jean-Claude Juncker's appointment (in February 2015) of former French foreign minister Michel Barnier as his defence advisor can be seen as an expression of the Commission's ambition in defence (EPSC, 2015). In its own communication prior to the meeting the Commission went a lot further than research, raising the possibility of EU-owned capabilities, which antagonized many Member States (European Commission, 2013). But why not allow the Commission to participate in capability projects as long as they are dual-use, with civilian as well as military applications? Most strategic enablers, which is where Europe is most deficient, are dual-use. An observation drone for example can monitor the EU's external borders, or refugee streams, or a natural disaster just as well as enemy forces in operations. Imagine that nine EU Member States would join up to build a drone. Why could the Commission not contribute as if it were a tenth Member State, contributing 10 per cent of the funds, and owning 10 per cent of the capacity afterwards, or even drawing rights for 10 per cent of its use? If this were done through the EDA, which is an intergovernmental agency, with the defence ministers of the Member States making up the board, they would not need to fear for their prerogatives. Ideas such as this ruffle a lot of feathers in the capitals, but the privilege of having your feathers ruffled comes with a price tag. Since most Member States do not have many funds available to invest, they would do well not to dismiss this option out of hand. There really are no reasons therefore to oppose pooling and sharing with the Commission. The only caveat is that Member States risk regarding EU funding as a substitute for national expenditure, but that can easily be avoided by putting a cap on the European share of the funding of any project. In this scenario, when the next CDP is being drafted, the Commission could give its own input on capability priorities alongside the Member States.

Payment schedules are at times even more crucial. One of the obstacles to multinational cooperation is that potential participating states rarely have budget available at the same time. Through the EDA, the European Investment Bank (EIB) could allow Member States to have their "European Defence Account" into which they could make down payments for a specific project as soon as it has been authorized by their political authorities. Thus Ministries of Defence could avoid falling victim to subsequent budget cuts or having to return allocated budgets to the Treasury if they have not been spent within the fiscal year. Member States could also borrow funds, in order not to miss the opportunity to join in a project while waiting for national funds to become available. In addition they could choose to spread the payment schedule over a longer period (even over the entire life-cycle of a project) if that were the only way in which they could participate.

Capability Development: Coordinating Clusters of Cooperation

In spite of all these very rational arguments, it remains difficult to convince states to invest in big multinational projects. The pressure on their defence budgets is pushing countries to cooperate in smaller, mostly regionally organized, clusters though. One of the reasons is that many states have reduced their forces to such an extent already that the classic way of cutting the defence budget, by shaving a little of every capability, no longer works. Many capabilities have already become so small in scale that any further reduction would simply kill them. Capitals are thus facing the qualitatively very different choice of which capabilities to maintain and which to scrap altogether. Cooperating with like-minded countries is then a way of creating the critical mass to maintain capabilities that have become unaffordable at the national level. Not to acquire strategic enablers though: the critical mass required to build a satellite or a drone is such that it requires an EU-level initiative with a dozen or more Member States, rather than a regional cluster of three or four. The two levels of defence cooperation are both necessary therefore.

The landscape of regional clusters is a very dynamic one (Pertusot, 2015), though more so in northern than in southern Europe. Most eye-catching is the Franco-British aim to establish a Combined Joint Expeditionary Force in the framework of their bilateral Lancaster House agreements. The Benelux, the Baltics, the Nordics, the Visegrad countries, the Dutch-German corps and others are all exploring ways of deepening cooperation. The acquisition of the A400M Airbus transport aircraft over the next years by several of the members of EATC will open opportunities to widen and deepen cooperation. Similarly, the ongoing replacement of fighter aircraft across Europe will create chances to renew or to start cooperation between those acquiring the same planes. Yet, with a few notable exceptions (such as Belgian-Dutch naval integration and EATC) cooperation is only skin-deep. In many clusters cooperation is limited to some coordination measures, to ad hoc procurement or to specific fields (such as education). To achieve really significant cost-savings, through synergies and effects of scale, real pooling and specialization is required. That means that even while manoeuvre units and platforms remain national, staffed by national personnel, all tasks relating to logistics, maintenance, training, and headquarters are either implemented by permanent multinational units (pooling) or are divided between the members of the cluster according to a fixed division of labour (specialization), and more capabilities are co-located on a reduced number of bases.

The Belgian-Dutch experience is evidence that such far-reaching yet flexible integration is perfectly viable. In this example, a ship either sails under Belgian flag and has a Belgian crew, or under a Dutch flag with a Dutch crew. But there is only one naval command and one naval operational school, while training, maintenance and logistics for the frigates is assured by the Netherlands for both countries' ships and vice versa for the mine hunters. If Belgium deploys a frigate for operation Atalanta, the Netherlands is in no way obliged to also send one; it just has to guarantee that the

Dutch staff in the support structures do their job. This model is easily transferrable to other capability areas, such as fighter aircraft.

In Wales in September 2014 NATO took a new step to promote such deep integration in clusters by endorsing the Framework Nations Concept (FNC). The idea of this initially German proposal is that several smaller nations "merge" their capabilities into those of one larger nation that still has a "comparatively broad capability spectrum" and provides the strategic enablers. This framework nation would coordinate capability development for the cluster as a whole, in function of NATO targets, and would have "coordination authority for planning and harmonization with NATO HQ" (Bundesministerium der Verteidigung, 2013). The intention to create three FNC clusters was announced in Wales. A German-led cluster of ten nations will focus on capability development in logistics, CBRN protection, delivering firepower from land, air and sea, and deployable headquarters. The UK concentrates on operations instead of capabilities, intending to establish a Joint Expeditionary Force capable of high-intensity operations by 2018, with Denmark, Estonia, Latvia, Lithuania, the Netherlands, and Norway. Italy is exploring the creation of a cluster with Albania, Croatia, Hungary, Slovenia and Austria, with a focus on stabilization and reconstruction, provision of enablers, usability of land formations and command and control. There are thus many interpretations of the FNC. Many in NATO headquarters see the FNC clusters as the basis from which to create the rotations of the VJTF, in which case they would almost exclusively serve Article 5 purposes.

The core of the FNC is that a group of nations turn around the prevailing mind-set. What mostly happens now is that countries plan separately for national capabilities and afterwards, if they so choose, explore the possibilities for cooperation. Obviously, many opportunities will then have been foreclosed. The FNC by contrast supposes that countries regard their capabilities in one or in a range of areas as constituting a single force, of which each offers a component, and therefore jointly plan for it as a single force from the start. This is in fact the logical end-state of ever-deepening cooperation. Belgian-Dutch naval cooperation has de facto reached this stage: integration has progressed so far that in practice it can no longer be undone, for neither nation could afford to reconstitute nationally the capabilities that have been pooled or in which the other has specialized. Henceforth they have no choice but to plan together, notably for the replacement of the frigates, if they want to maintain the degree of pooling and specialization. The Belgian-Dutch example thus demonstrates that far-reaching cooperation can be achieved in any cluster, including between smaller countries, and does not necessarily require smaller nations to plug into one framework nation.

All of this has been attempted before, actually, in the EU: Permanent Structured Cooperation (PESCO), which the Lisbon Treaty sought to introduce but was never implemented, envisaged exactly the same. The idea was that a core group of EU Member States would increase their capabilities by cooperating more closely and, just like the Eurozone countries, fulfil certain criteria as regards their defence effort. Those criteria, defined in Article 2 of the Protocol on PESCO attached to the Treaty on European Union included: "bring[ing] their defence apparatus into line with each other as far as possible", agreeing a level of investment in defence equipment, and participating in EDA projects. Following the classic spill-over logic of functional integration, this would have led participating Member States first to focus their limited budgetary margin on the projects agreed on in PESCO and, gradually, to plan together in order to maximize synergies. Following an exploratory seminar under the Spanish EU Presidency, the Belgian Presidency in the second half of 2010 (with which I had the chance to cooperate closely) made clear proposals on how to implement PESCO, but we soon realized that most other Member States were doubting whether it needed to be implemented at all. The issue was therefore circumvented by launching voluntary Pooling and Sharing (Biscop and Coelmont, 2011).

If some countries now want to attempt similarly far-reaching military integration in a NATO context, that can only be applauded. But just as for PESCO, the participants will have to muster the will to revisit their national defence planning without any taboos, to do away with national capability initiatives proven to be redundant, to pool and to specialize in order to generate savings, and to contribute their fair share (in function of GDP) to the projects launched to fill the capability shortfalls. In other words, for the FNC to have added value when compared to existing clusters of defence cooperation, the three emerging FNC clusters must really be as ambitious as the original German proposal. Europe is not lacking in schemes for defence cooperation; the issue is that most do not lead to permanent pooling and specialization and thus have but a marginal impact on Europe's problems of fragmentation, redundancies, and shortfalls.

There is one obvious difference between the FNC and PESCO: there would have been only one PESCO, but there are already three FNC clusters in the making, all of which have a very different view of what a Framework Nation is supposed to do. That need not be problematic, but it points once again to the crucial importance of coordination. The single most important lesson learned from two decades of European defence cooperation is that bottom-up initiatives by the countries alone do not suffice. Of course neither NATO nor the EU can oblige their Member States to make specific defence choices. But they must coordinate the multitudinous initiatives, by individual countries as well as by clusters, which make up the landscape of European defence. Otherwise new duplications will simply arise, not between countries but between clusters, while there is no guarantee that their spontaneous bottom-up initiatives will effectively address all of the priority shortfalls. If coordination could be called the first principle of clustering, then the second must be non-exclusivity. The aim is not to create self-sufficient and exclusive "islands of cooperation" (Valasek, 2011), with each cluster of countries providing the full spectrum of capabilities and with each nation participating in only one cluster. That would hinder rather than promote expeditionary operations, by reducing countries' options for deployment to only one framework. And it is an illusion anyway, for as already stated, acquiring the strategic enablers that Europe is lacking requires a critical mass that surpasses the capacity of any cluster.

Ultimately, European defence will be a complex puzzle of capabilities mustered at the national, cluster, EU and NATO levels. The clusters will be overlapping: each country will join various clusters, in function of the capability areas in which it wants to remain active. This is already the case today: Belgium for example has integrated its navy with the Netherlands, but trains its pilots in France, pools its air transport fleet via EATC, and is a member of the Eurocorps in which the Netherlands does not participate. The EU is the level at which the strategic enablers will be developed and acquired, each by a single cluster coordinated by the EDA, in which most or all Europeans (and ideally the Commission) participate. NATO will likely limit its multinational capability development efforts to areas related to territorial defence and that require a contribution from both sides of the Atlantic. Without top-down coordination, there can be no certainty that initiatives at all these levels are even attempting to build the same puzzle, let alone that all pieces of the puzzle are there and that not too many pieces exist more than once. Hence the need for a revised Headline Goal to frame European defence cooperation.

Yes, this will be very complex – inevitably so. When in 2015 he made a sudden plea for one European army, Commission President Juncker was of course right in principle, and his call was echoed by several experts (CEPS, 2015; Juncker, 2015). If tomorrow I would be given the €160 billion that the EU Member States now spend on defence with the assignment to ensure the defence of Europe, I would of course build one army, navy and air force, not 28. This is like the gentleman who gets lost in the countryside and after hours of desperate wandering finally stumbles upon a farmer, whom he asks how to get back to the capital, and receives the answer: I would not start from here. But here we are, with 28 sets of armed forces rather than one, and we have to move on from here. Regional clusters and EDA projects are the way forward. One can note though that the countries that appear most willing are the Benelux, France and Germany, in various constellations. Perhaps, if they would link the different clusters in which they take part together, and if they would all contribute their share to the big EDA projects, a core group could emerge. This could be a de facto PESCO: without activating the Protocol, an informal core group could achieve the same thing of eventually moving from pooling of national efforts to planning, from the start, for a truly multinational effort.

Conclusion

The US pivot has already altered the nature of the European security architecture. As Europeans assume more responsibility and increasingly act as security providers, so the nature of the relationship between the EU and NATO will automatically evolve further. As it stands today, "to hand a problem to NATO is simply to hand it back to the United States" (Posen, 2014, p. 39). But as the US is less and less willing to accept this, NATO will have a European future or not much of a future at all.

Europe's strategic situation demands a review of the defence posture of the European allies and partners/EU Member States. For as the neighbourhood that Europe has to care about is expanding and the challenges multiplying, so its American ally's political and military commitment is declining. The first step therefore is that the "European bloc" has to decide which responsibilities it wants to assume as a security provider outside its borders, and translate that into capability targets that allow for the "bloc" to act fully autonomously, without the US, when necessary. The EU is best placed to express that ambition, through the European Council, and to detail its capability implications for expeditionary operations, through the EDA. NATO can then integrate these target for autonomous European expeditionary action in the overall capability targets for Europeans, including their collective defence obligations, through the NDPP. The EU High Representative, Federica Mogherini, who is also the head of the EDA, and the NATO Secretary-General, Jens Stoltenberg, could appeal to European nations together and publish a joint statement urging them to participate in EDA projects as an indispensable way of meeting their commitments in NATO. They could even go one step further and produce one integrated list of priority projects (notably strategic enablers) for the European allies and partners/EU Member States, thus ending once and for all the beauty contest between the two organizations that has been a stumbling block all along on the road to effective cooperation. This may appear a small step, but it would do away with an excuse that Member States abuse all too often in order to mask their lack of delivery in either organization. Once settled on the priorities, the EDA is best placed to be the "architect" of cooperation to develop and acquire these priority capabilities together. Bringing these capabilities up to standard through manoeuvres is best done through the NATO command structure, so as to ensure interoperability among European forces and between them and the other Allies.

In an actual crisis situation the EU is the better forum to take the political initiative: assessing its importance, deciding which response is required, and forging the coalition that can deliver it. The response can then be framed in the broader context of the EU's grand strategy and its regional and country strategies, and can be designed in a comprehensive way, making optimal use of the broad range of diplomatic and economic instruments (and means) that are only available at the EU-level. Neither NATO nor an ad hoc coalition can offer this. Of course, if in a given crisis the EU takes the political decision to respond militarily, it need not necessarily act through its own CSDP; in many cases NATO or even an ad hoc coalition will be the preferred option. Europeans will likely avail themselves of the NATO command structure in most scenarios demanding large scale, high intensity military intervention. If the EU is the most suitable strategic and political forum for comprehensive crisis management, the appropriate military command structure can only be selected on a case-by-case basis, in function of the characteristics of the crisis.

Coordination, cooperation and eventually integration: those are the keys to build an affordable and coherent set of European forces. Ultimately however, without a much more specific and explicit European statement of political and military ambition, cooperation will remain rudderless. Once again, strategy is the answer.

Conclusion

"Europe has never been so prosperous, so secure nor so free". The opening sentence of the 2003 European Security Strategy is often quoted with derision, as obvious proof of its obsolescence. Yet I challenge the reader to name a period in time when the countries of the EU were more prosperous, secure or free than today. In the light of history, the bold opening statement of the ESS still holds true. European integration, "simultaneously the dullest and most daring trick that statesmen had ever attempted" (Morris, 2014, p. 342), works.

What has changed since 2003 is, first of all, that although Europe still is one of the most prosperous places on the planet, it has become more unequal, as a consequence of the financial crisis and the way it was addressed. Thanks to the buffer provided by the European social model, inequality has risen less than in the US, but it has risen, in some Member States dramatically so – because the European Commission and the IMF forced them to dismantle the social model. Inequality is dangerous. First because the egalitarian aspiration is precisely what binds most Europeans to their states and to the European project on which they have embarked, rather than nationalism or great power ambitions. Second because the egalitarian aspiration is at the heart of what makes Europe an inspiring place to many people in other parts of the world; it is the source of Europe's soft power.

The other change is that Europeans have learned again from the turmoil in their neighbourhood and the terrorist attacks on their soil what they should have known all along: that their freedom and security are not self-evident. Europeans are very fortunate that among themselves, within their Union, they need no longer think about geopolitics and count tanks, fighter aircraft and battleships. But that should not blind them to the fact that outside the EU geopolitics still matter. Europe just cannot "see itself in insular terms, cocooned from the great power rivalries emerging in the Pacific, and clothed in a regional bubble of atypical but seemingly eternal security", as Strachan (2013, p. 127) fears. If it does not take into account the geopolitical situation and prioritizes the most important challenges to European interests, Europe's distinctive preventive, comprehensive and multilateral foreign policy will not succeed.

The response to these two changes must be optimism. The optimist may be proven wrong, but at least he will have enjoyed life until then – there is no need to be pre-emptively unhappy. Gloom and doom rarely generate inspiration. An optimist message about investment, job creation, and how to perfect the social model (rather than about its defects) is the only way of restoring confidence within Europe itself. A self-confident Europe can in turn engage with the world, advertising its model of society, working with those who share its egalitarian aspiration, and acting against those who go too far in breaking the rules.

That does require strategy. "Having a strategy suggests an ability to look up from the short term and the trivial to view the long term and the essential, to address causes rather than symptoms, to see woods rather than trees", says Lawrence Freedman (2013, p. ix). There are several woods around Europe, and jungles, and mountains and deserts, so strategizing is difficult. Even more or so for a complex composite actor like the EU which, as Jolyon Howorth (2014, p. 221) eloquently puts it, is more used to "bargains and compromises: a little bit of this for the Greeks and a little bit of that for the Poles" than to the "bold decision-making and implementation" that grand strategy requires. I do not want to overstate the importance of strategy either. Unfortunately for us academics who write books, it is not because it is written down that it will be so, not even if the European Council endorses it. Having a strategy does not guarantee success, for other actors will obviously be pursuing a strategy of their own that may be at odds with yours. Nor does not having a strategy guarantee failure, as others may act even less soundly than you. And you can simply get lucky, of course. "I know he's a good general, but is he lucky?", Napoleon is reputed to have asked. Bad generals and strategists rarely stay lucky for long though. You cannot be half strategic. Either you know what you want and you act accordingly, or you do not.

References

Ali, Tariq (2015), "The New World Disorder", *The London Review of Books*, 37:7: 19–22.

Ashton, Catherine (2013), *Preparing the December 2013 European Council on Security and Defence. Final Report by the High Representative/Head of the EDA on the Common Security and Defence Policy*. Brussels, 15 October.

Berlin, Isaiah (1998), "Two Concepts of Liberty", in *The Proper Study of Mankind: An Anthology of Essays*, edited by Henry Hardy and Roger Hausheer. London: Pimlico.

Biscop, Sven (2012), "The UK and European Defence: Leading or Leaving?", *International Affairs*, 88:6: 1297–313.

—— (2013), "Peace without Money, War without Americans: Challenges for European Strategy", *International Affairs*, 89:5: 1125–42.

Biscop, Sven and Jan Joel Andersson (2008) (eds), *The EU and the European Security Strategy. Forging a Global Europe*. Abingdon: Routledge.

Biscop, Sven and Jo Coelmont (2011), "CSDP and the Ghent Framework: The Indirect Approach to Permanent Structured Cooperation?", *European Foreign Affairs Review*, 16:2: 149–67.

—— (2012), *Europe, Strategy and Armed Forces: The Making of a Distinctive Power*. Abingdon: Routledge.

Brands, Hal (2014), *What Good is Grand Strategy? Power and Purpose in American Statecraft from Harry S. Truman to George W. Bush*. Ithaca, NY: Cornell University Press.

Bundesministerium der Verteidigung (2013), *Food for Thought. Framework Nations Concept*. Berlin.

CEPS (2015), *More Union in European Defence*. Brussels: Centre for European Policy Studies.

Coelmont, Jo (2009), *End-State Afghanistan*. Egmont Paper 29. Brussels: Egmont Institute.

Coelmont, Jo and Sven Biscop (2014), *Building European Defence: An Architect and a Bank*. Security Policy Brief 56. Brussels: Egmont Institute.

Coll, Steve (2013), "Hard on Obama", *The New York Review of Books*, 60:12.

Coolsaet, Rik (2015), *What Drives Europeans to Syria, and to IS? Insights from the Belgian Case*. Egmont Paper No. 75. Brussels: Egmont Institute.

Cooper, Robert (2004), *The Breaking of Nations: Order and Chaos in the Twenty-First Century*. London: Atlantic Books.

Council of the European Union (2011a), *Strategic Framework for the Horn of Africa*. Brussels, 11 November.

—— (2011b), *Strategy for Security and Development in the Sahel*. Brussels, 21 March.

—— (2014a), *European Union Maritime Security Strategy*. Brussels, 24 June.

—— (2014b), *Policy Framework for Systematic and Long-term Defence Cooperation*. Brussels, 18 November.

de France, Olivier (2015), "France and the CSDP: A Tin of Paint and a Can of Worms", *European Geostrategy*, 7 January. Retrieved from www.europeangeostrategy. org.

Department of Defence (2012), *Sustaining US Global Leadership: Priorities for 21st Century Defense*. Washington.

Doyle, Michael W. (2015), *The Question of Intervention. John Stuart Mill & the Responsibility to Protect*. New Haven, CT: Yale University Press.

EPSC (2015), *In Defence of Europe. Defence Integration as a Response to Europe's Strategic Moment*. EPSC Strategic Notes Issue 4. Brussels: European Political Strategy Centre.

EUISS (2013), *Back from the Future. European Military Capabilities Horizon 2025: Options and Implications*. Paris: EU Institute for Security Studies.

European Commission (2013), *Towards a More Competitive and Efficient Defence and Security Sector?* COM (2013) 542 final. Brussels, 24 July.

—— (2015), *Towards a New Neighbourhood Policy. Joint Consultation Paper*. JOIN (2015) 6 final. Brussels, 4 March.

European Council (2003), *European Security Strategy. A Secure Europe in a Better World*. Brussels, 12 December.

—— (2008), *Report on the Implementation of the European Security Strategy. Providing Security in a Changing World*. Brussels, 11 December.

—— (2013), *Conclusions*. Brussels, 19–20 December.

—— (2015), *Conclusions*. Brussels, 25–26 June.

European Defence Agency (2014), *Future Capabilities: Emerging Trends and Key Priorities*. Brussels.

Freedman, Lawrence (2013), *Strategy*. Oxford: Oxford University Press.

Future of Europe Group (2012), *Final Report*. Foreign Ministers of Austria, Belgium, Denmark, France, Italy, Germany, Luxembourg, the Netherlands, Portugal, Poland and Spain, 17 September.

Gaddis, John Lewis (2011), *George F. Kennan: An American Life*. New York: Penguin.

Gray, Colin S. (2010), *The Strategy Bridge: Theory for Practice*. Oxford: Oxford University Press.

Grevi, Giovanni (2009), *The Interpolar World: A New Scenario*. Occasional Paper No. 79. Paris: EU Institute for Security Studies.

Her Majesty's Government (2010), *Securing Britain in an Age of Uncertainty: The Strategic Defence and Security Review*. London.

Howorth, Jolyon (2014), *Security and Defence Policy in the European Union. Second Edition*. Basingstoke: Palgrave.

Hunter, Robert (2009), "NATO's Strategic Focus: Satisfying All of the Allies", *American Foreign Policy Interests*, 31: 78–89.

Judt, Tony (2005), *Postwar: A History of Europe Since 1945*. London: Penguin.

—— (2008), *Reappraisals: Reflections on the Forgotten 21st Century*. London: Penguin Books.

—— (2010), *Ill Fares the Land: A Treatise on our Present Discontents*. London: Allen Lane.

Juncker, Jean-Claude (2015), "Halten sie sich an Frau Merkel". Ich mache das! *Die Welt am Sonntag*, 8 March.

Krugman, Paul (2012), *End this Depression Now!* New York: Norton.

Lehne, Stefan (2008), *Time to Reset the European Neighbourhood Policy*. Brussels: Carnegie-Europe.

Lord Tennyson, Alfred (1854). "The Charge of the Light Brigade". Available at: http://www.poetryfoundation.org/poem/174586. Accessed: 17th September 2015.

Major, Claudia and Christian Mölling (2014), *The Framework Nations Concept. Germany's Contribution to a Capable European Defence*. SWP Comments 52. Berlin: Stifting Wissenschaft und Politik.

Michaels, Jeffrey H. (2014), *America's Global Defence Predicament*. Egmont Paper 72. Brussels: Egmont Institute.

Ministère de la Défense (2013), *Livre blanc sur la défense et la sécurité nationale*. Paris.

Mogherini, Federica (2015a), *Keynote Speech at Chatham House*, 24 February 2015. Retrieved from www.eeas.europa.eu.

—— (2015b), *The European Union in a Changing Global Environment. A More Connected, Contested and Complex World*. Brussel: EEAS.

Morris, Ian (2010), *Why the West Rules – For Now. The Patterns of History, and What They Reveal About the Future*. New York: Farrar, Straus and Giroux.

—— (2014), *War: What is it Good for? The Role of Conflict in Civilization, from Primates to Robots*. London: Profile Books.

NATO (2014), *Wales summit declaration issued by the Heads of State and Government participating in the meeting of the North Atlantic Council in Wales*. 5 September.

Pertusot, Vivien (2015), "Défense européenne: enfin du nouveau", *Politique Étrangère*, 80:2: 11–23.

Posen, Barry R. (2014), *Restraint. A New Foundation for US Grand Strategy*. Ithaca, NY: Cornell University Press.

Renard, Thomas (2015), *The Asian Infrastructure Investment Bank: China's New Multilateralism and the Erosion of the West*. Security Policy Brief No. 63. Brussels: Egmont.

Shea, Jamie (2013), "NATO post-2014: Preserving the Essentials", in *The State of Defence in Europe: State of Emergency?*, edited by Sven Biscop and Daniel Fiott. Egmont Paper 62. Brussels: Egmont Institute, pp. 27–32.

Simón, Luis (2012), "CSDP, Strategy and Crisis Management: Out of Area or Out of Business", *The International Spectator*, 47:3: 100–15.

Stiglitz, Joseph E. (2012), *The Price of Inequality: How Today's Divided Society Endangers our Future*. New York: Norton.

Strachan, Hew (2013), *The Direction of War. Contemporary Strategy in Historical Perspective*. Cambridge: Cambridge University Press.

The White House (2002), *The National Security Strategy of the United States of America*. Washington, September.

—— (2015), *National Security Strategy*. Washington, February.

Thyssen, Marianne (2015), *Policy Orientations for a Social Europe*. Remarks, Strasbourg, European Parliament, 9 June.

Trevor-Roper, Hugh (1947), *The Last Days of Hitler*. New York: Macmillan.

—— (2014), *One Hundred Letters*, edited by Richard Davenport-Hines and Adam Sisman. Oxford: Oxford University Press.

UI, PISM, IAI and Elcano (2013), *Towards a European Global Strategy. Securing European Influence in a Changing World*. Stockholm, Warsaw, Rome and Madrid, 28 May.

Valasek, Tomas (2011), *Surviving Austerity: The Case for a New Approach to EU Military Cooperation*. London: Centre for European Reform.

Wilkinson, Richard G. and Kate Pickett (2009), *The Spirit Level: Why More Equal Societies Almost Always Do Better*. London: Allen Lane.

Wood, Tony (2014), "Back from the Edge? On the Situation in Ukraine", *London Review of Books*, 36:11: 37–8.

Youngs, Richard (2014), *The Uncertain Legacy of Crisis. European Foreign Policy Faces the Future*. Washington: Carnegie Endowment for International Peace.